The Entrepreneur

The Entrepreneur
Eight Case Studies

Edited by
RICHARD LYNN

London · George Allen & Unwin Ltd

Ruskin House   Museum Street

Printed in Great Britain
in 11 point Times Roman type
by Unwin Brothers Limited
The Gresham Press
Old Woking, Surrey, England

Contents

1 Introduction: The Entrepreneur

RICHARD LYNN

There are numerous people who have thought of setting up their own business. To succeed as an entrepreneur brings great rewards. These rewards are partly financial but are also much wider than this. They bring the satisfaction of having built something by one's own efforts, of independence, and of a sense of serving the community, because the entrepreneur can only succeed through satisfying the needs of his fellow men more efficiently.

But to try to start up a new business involves risks, and the prospects of giving up a safe job with a secure salary are daunting. How is a successful new business established, what are the problems encountered and how can they be solved? Little has been written to give guidance to those who are considering whether they should launch themselves on a career as an entrepreneur. It is to help such people that this book has been written. It consists of the accounts of men who have set up their own businesses from nothing or from very modest beginnings. In some cases the entrepreneurs tell their own stories while in others I have written up the accounts from interviews and records.

The entrepreneurs whose stories are told have been chosen to represent a wide cross section of different types of business. The first story is told by Mr Ralph Hilton who built up a firm in one of the most traditional of all services, the transportation of goods. Mr Dermot Ryan chose one of the growing service industries, car hire. Mr Vladimir Raitz developed the charter holiday. Mr Colin Chapman found a niche in a seemingly impregnable mass production industry, car manufacture. Mr Tom Land has worked in advanced technology. Mr Bernard Matthews has built his business in satisfying what is perhaps the most fundamental of all human needs—food. At the other extreme, Mr Nigel Vinson went into a new industry, plastics; and finally, Mr Jack Dickman has built a company in a field which combines entertainment and advanced technology—radios, record players and related products. The moral of this wide variety of areas in which business success has been achieved is surely clear. It is that it is possible to build a successful business in any field of human activity, only provided that you have the will to succeed.

THE PSYCHOLOGY OF THE ENTREPRENEUR

One of the first questions an intending entrepreneur may want to ask himself is whether he has the right personality qualities for success in running a business of his own. There are several personality qualities that are useful. Probably the most important is motivation or energy. This is something the entrepreneur must have if he is to succeed. Mr Dickman puts it bluntly in his chapter on his company Fidelity Radio when he says that in the early days he worked sixteen hours a day, seven days a week. This degree of dedication is certainly not strictly necessary. But a strong drive for success is undoubtedly essential to build up a business of any magnitude. It is no good being half-hearted about it.

Where this drive for success comes from and what precisely it is, are complex problems. What is fairly certain is that the motivation may come from several sources. Undoubtedly one of the most obvious is the desire to make money. The rate of taxation in Britain on salaries is so severe beyond around £5,000 a year that it is impossible to make a fortune as an employee. But it can still be done through setting up one's own business. Once it is successfully established it can be sold, or partly sold by selling off some of the shares. The entrepreneur then obtains a sum of money on which capital gains tax will be levied, but this is comparatively light and there will be a substantial sum left to the entrepreneur. Most entrepreneurs take at least some of their money out of their companies in this way.

But the desire to make a fortune is by no means the only motive for entrepreneurship and in many cases is probably not the most important. One of the chief motives for many entrepreneurs has been the desire for independence. It is a great thing to be one's own boss. There are some people who find it hard to bear being directed by superiors, to whom one has to submit as an employee, and the only way of escaping this is through setting up one's own business.

In the late 1940s a study was carried out in Chicago of 120 men who had set up as entrepreneurs. The conclusion of the investigators, Drs Collins, Moore and Unwalla, was that the entrepreneurs had been motivated chiefly by this desire for independence. The reverse side of the coin was a dislike of being under the authority of others, and many of the entrepreneurs had shown this trait from quite early in life. They had not got on well with their fathers, schoolmasters or, when they took a job, bosses, and eventually realised that life would only be tolerable if they could be free from the authority of the boss. This drove them into entrepreneurship.

This is certainly quite a common reason for motivating men to set up their own businesses, but this does not exhaust the motives. One of the leading psychologists of entrepreneurship, Dr D. C. McClelland, maintains that a strong 'achievement motive' is what tends to drive men to become entrepreneurs. The achievement motive is more or less the same as the creative urge and the person who has it has two attributes. He likes both to do a job well as an end in itself and also to do it well in competition with others. The appeal of entrepreneurship to people with strong achievement motives is that in running your own business there is great scope for achievement. In most occupations the rewards for success are rather intangible. Normally you move up a hierarchy and are rewarded by a higher salary and greater status. In many jobs it is difficult to tell whether what you are doing is really having much effect. For instance, the teacher has little idea of the long-term effects of his work and whether his efforts have been worth while or not. A judge who passes a sentence cannot tell whether he is doing anything to reform the convicted man or to deter others from committing crimes. And this lack of certainty about whether your endeavours are having much effect is present in many occupations.

This certainty that you have succeeded—or failed—is one of the pleasures of being an entrepreneur. The success of your business is measured by whether or not you have made money. And you can tell by looking at your bank statements whether or not you have been successful.

But let us be quite clear about this. For many entrepreneurs it is not the money as such that is particularly important. The making of money is important because it is a symbol of success. The criterion of success in business is largely, if not necessarily entirely, the profitability of the company. Thus high profits prove that you have done the job well. They are also quite nice to have for the ordinary purposes of life.

For many entrepreneurs the basic drive is creative, to build something out of nothing. In many ways this drive resembles the motivation of the creative scientist and artist. The creative scientist and artist are doing something new. They have first to create some new entity in the imagination and must then apply certain techniques for transforming this imagined entity into reality. Finally, the reward is the satisfaction of seeing the entity in existence, created by himself. And exactly the same creative processes, from original conception to final product, take place in the entrepreneur. The really great entrepreneurs, like the greatest scientists and artists, hit on something new. Henry Ford could imagine a future in which quite ordinary middle-class people drove cars. Sir Billy Butlin must have had a vision of the English enjoying themselves in regimented holiday camps. But it is not necessary to have a new vision of this type to be a competent and successful entrepreneur, any more than it is to be a competent and successful scientist or artist. In any case, Edison was surely right when he said that genius is 99 per cent perspiration. To which we may add that 100 per cent perspiration will take you a long way.

Strong motivation, then, is probably the single most important quality that an entrepreneur must have. The motivation can be of different kinds. Whatever the motivation may be, if the intending entrepreneur has this motivation to succeed, what else is necessary? Reasonable intelligence, an ability to work with others, and general business competence are probably the most important requirements. There is no reason why anyone who has these, together with the motivation, should not become a successful entrepreneur.

THE PRODUCT OR SERVICE

The first thing that the intending entrepreneur has to decide about is the product or service. The great entrepreneurs of history are generally men who have invented and produced a new product—James Watt's steam engine, Henry Ford's mass-produced car, Gillette's safety razor and so forth. Today entrepreneurs are still developing businesses on the basis of a new invention. One of the best examples in the post World War II period is Mr John Odell and Mr Leslie Smith's company Lesney Products. This is the company that makes the matchbox toy cars. The company is based on a new method of die-casting zinc alloy devised by Mr Odell and Mr Smith. The method produces a cast with much finer detail than had been possible hitherto. This invention was the basis of the considerable success of the company.

Several of the entrepreneurs who tell their stories in this book have built up their businesses on the basis of new inventions. Mr Dickman of Fidelity Radio devised a new technique for moulding plastic casings for tape recorders. Mr Vinson of Plastic Coatings has devised his own machinery for dipping materials into plastic.

But it is by no means essential to develop a new product to be a successful entrepreneur, and probably most entrepreneurs do not build up their companies on the basis of a new invention. Indeed, it is often safer to enter a field where the initial teething troubles have been tested by others. One can point here to the great successes of Japanese companies in recent years, which have been largely based on making and selling cheaply and efficiently products developed in other countries, such as ships, cars, motor cycles, electronic equipment and so forth.

It is, however, desirable to try to select a product which seems likely to have an expanding future. A good example is Mr Vinson's choice of plastics when he first set up his business in 1952. Another is Mr Raitz's choice of the package holiday business. Obviously it would not be sensible to try to start up a new business in a declining industry.

Becoming an entrepreneur is generally associated with making and selling a product. But today the greatest expansion of entrepreneurial activities is in selling a service rather than a product, and it is probably here that the greatest scope for setting up a business lies. The reason for this is that manufacturing industry is generally more efficient if it can be done on a large scale and this generally requires too much capital for an entrepreneur. Indeed, this can also become true of some service industries. Mr Raitz describes how it would be impossible for someone to enter the package holiday business today on £3,000, as he did in 1949. And Mr Hilton points out that it would be equally impossible to enter the transportation business today with no capital whatever, which was how he began shortly after the end of World War II.

There have been many successful service businesses established over the last twenty years or so. Launderettes, accommodation bureaux, employment agencies and holiday travel firms are perhaps some of the most striking examples. Another, of which an account is given by Mr Dermot Ryan, is the car hire business.

Naturally the entrepreneur who thinks of something new has some advantage over the man who copies an existing product or service. On the other hand, he is also taking a bigger risk, unless perhaps he has some special technological expertise which gives him a lead over his competitors. For those without such expertise, there is much to be said for starting with some fairly safe product or service that seems likely to have an expanding future.

FINANCE

Once the product or service has been decided upon, the next problem is money. The entrepreneur will almost certainly have to reckon on finding some money of his own before he can expect to borrow from others. His own stake will probably come either from personal saving or perhaps from borrowing from members of his family. But for many businesses the initial capital need not be large. A few hundred pounds will be sufficient for a start. It is even possible to start with nothing whatever as was the case with Mr Hilton. Once some money has been found and a business plan drawn up, the entrepreneur will be able to approach various sources of finance for loans. The best to try first are the ordinary clearing banks. Their rates of interest are the lowest and the procedures for getting a loan are simple. When requesting a loan from the bank manager it is important to have one's business plans, financial requirements and repayment proposals well thought out. They should be prepared and typed professionally. The banks will normally require the loan to be repaid over a period of several years, and if the loan is obtained it is important to meet the commitments one has entered into. The bank manager then acquires confidence in one's reliability and will generally advance greater sums in the future. If the business prospers it should not be difficult to get larger overdraft facilities agreed from year to year.

It is well to remember that the banks are frequently subjected to credit squeezes in which they are not able to lend further sums. They may even require the overdraft to be reduced by a small percentage. These credit squeezes do not last indefinitely and when they are eased is the time to approach the bank manager. One should then be able to acquire a loan for a period of five years or so which will not be affected by the next squeeze. If the British banks will not lend, it may be worth trying some of the foreign clearing banks, such as the American ones, which have branches in Britain.

Once a business is well established there are various institutions which will provide further finance. When a business is reasonably sizeable the merchant banks will finance expansion which they consider sound. Generally they take a minority shareholding and look forward to the company going public in due course, so that they can then sell their shares on the open market and get their money back. Some entrepreneurs dislike selling shares because they feel they are losing control of the company and hence losing their independence. But for the moderate-sized private company only a minority of shares need be sold to the merchant banks or other financial institutions. Control need not be lost. On the other hand, many entrepreneurs like to sell a proportion of their shares in order to obtain cash for various purposes, such as to give to their wives and children, to buy expensive houses and yachts or for other purposes which we need not go into here. Entrepreneurs' preferences differ on this matter. Among our own entrepreneurs, Mr Dickman of Fidelity Radios has sold or given away almost all his shares. He is happy with the £1 million odd he has made. On the other hand, Mr Raitz of Horizon Holidays has kept his entire shareholding. Mr Raitz, however, is exceptional and most entrepreneurs will probably find that as they expand they will have to sell a certain proportion of their shares.

Other sources of finance for an established business are the Charterhouse Industrial Development Company and the Industrial and Commercial Finance Corporation. They lend sums ranging between £5,000 and £500,000.

There are also a variety of grants available from the government for specific purposes, such as starting up a business in development areas, market research, overseas trade promotions and so forth. These Government schemes tend to change from time to time, and advice on the current position can be obtained from the CBI or from local authorities.

THE MECHANICS OF STARTING A COMPANY

There are certain mechanics to starting one's own business which can be dealt with briefly. It is generally considered best to set up a limited company, but the taxation laws change quite frequently and it will be best to seek the advice of an accountant at the time of starting. Limited companies can be bought off the hook quite cheaply and advertisements for them are found in *The Financial Times* and other quality newspapers. An alternative is to buy an existing business, which has the advantages that one is getting a going concern with premises, staff and customers, but the cost is greater except in rather rare cases where it may be possible to buy a concern below its asset value.

When the company is set up or bought, it is important for it to have a solicitor and an accountant. It may also be valuable to bring in an advisor as a non-executive director. He can be paid a few hundred pounds a year and, if the right man can be found, can be a source of useful advice. A retired entrepreneur who has experience of the many problems of setting up and running a small business would be a good person for this position.

An accountant is an especially useful person. The company's profitability will depend a good deal on making the most favourable arrangements from the point of view of taxation, and the entrepreneur should seek advice from an accountant. It is well to remember that accountants, like other people, differ considerably one from another in their competence. This is of course true of all professional men with apparently identical qualifications, but is perhaps especially true of accountants. It is worth taking some trouble to find a good one. Perhaps the best strategy is for the entrepreneur to learn a bit of company tax law himself and try out various proposals on his accountant. He will then learn how alert his accountant is.

STAFF SELECTION

The quality of the staff which the entrepreneur takes on at the initial stages is important. Although wage rates are fairly uniform for all workers in a particular trade, the quality of the work which people actually do varies considerably. The entrepreneur is well placed to take advantage of this fact. There are considerable differences in efficiency between different workers. This was demonstrated quite early in the century by the American industrial psychologist F. W.

B

Taylor. He investigated the process of loading and unloading pig-iron in the Bethlehem Steel Company. In the average plant, seventy-five men did this work and each shifted about $12\frac{1}{2}$ tons of pig-iron a day. Taylor selected one man called Schmidt who was particularly robust and experimented with different kinds of loading methods, using different sizes of shovel and so forth. He soon had Schmidt moving $47\frac{1}{2}$ tons a day instead of the $12\frac{1}{2}$ shifted by the average labourer. Most workers were simply incapable of doing anything like this amount of work, no matter what training was given them.

The company put into practice the logic of Taylor's investigation, which is of course to employ only men like Schmidt. They were able to reduce the number of men employed to nearly a quarter and pay 60 per cent higher wages to those who remained. This reduced the wage bill to around 30 per cent of its former size and greatly increased profitability.

Everyone will know from their everyday experience that Taylor's discovery applies very widely to many different occupations. Thus charwomen are generally paid at a standard rate in a particular area, but some charwomen are much better than others; typists are paid a fairly standard wage, but some type fast and accurately while others type slowly and inaccurately; and so on.

Recognition of wide differences between people in efficiency is resisted by employees, who exert strong pressure through their trade unions or professional associations for equal or approximately equal wage rates or salaries. The strength of the unions makes it impossible for the large company to take advantage of differences in efficiency by selecting and retaining only the most efficient workers and getting rid of the least efficient. But in the small firm the unions are much weaker or non-existent and the entrepreneur can do this. He has the advantages of flexibility possessed by the small English ships when they fought the great galleons of the Spanish armada.

For building up a workforce of efficient employees three principles must be used. The selection procedures must be good. It is not easy to select the right person and the best guide is to see the quality of their work, rather than talking to them and trying to form an impression of their capability. The second principle is that once they have been selected and have proved their worth they have to be given incentives to stay with the firm. We shall be considering this later under the heading of 'morale'. And thirdly, if the people selected turn out to be inefficient, they have to be dismissed. The problems of building up an efficient workforce are largely a matter of trial and error, hiring and firing different men until eventually the firm gets a good team. It is worth the entrepreneur's while to take a good deal of trouble over building up and keeping a good team, because once he succeeds in this he has a considerable advantage over his larger competitors.

MORALE

It is important to have a high level of morale in the business. The importance of good morale if an organisation is to perform efficiently seems to have been first appreciated in armies—no doubt because the penalties for having low morale are more severe than in civilian life. An army with high morale can be low in numbers, poorly fed and equipped, untrained, and yet defeat opponents apparently superior in every way.

The morale in an organisation is not an easy quality to define and measure, even though it may be agreed that it is important. While many definitions of morale have been proposed at various times, probably as straightforward and simple a one as any is that it consists of the feeling that the organisation one belongs to is a good one. This feeling has been described in various ways. Some writers have used the expression 'pride in the working group', and another term is 'esprit de corps'. It has been shown that organisations operate more efficiently when morale is high, e.g. by N. Walker in his book *Morale in the Civil Service*.

How is high morale to be achieved? A great deal depends upon the character and personality of the head of the organisation. Anyone who has worked in an organisation will know that its whole character is affected by the man at the top. Only if he has the right qualities will morale be high. But what are these qualities? The first are personal dedication and efficiency. If the leader is cynical or casual, or is inefficient and does not know as much as he should know about the job, his attitude infects the whole of the organisation. If the organisation is a commercial one it can hardly survive a head of this kind. The type is more often encountered in non-commercial organisations and the effect on morale is very bad.

It may probably be taken for granted that the entrepreneur will possess both dedication and competence and it will only be when we come to the entrepreneur's son or grandson that these qualities may be lacking. But these problems need not detain us and we may pass on to other ways of fostering good morale.

The way the head of the organisation treats his workforce is of the utmost importance. As a general principle, it may be useful to bear in mind that the head of an organisation should behave rather like a sensible father of a family. He should be kind, sympathetic, understanding and helpful, but at the same time he must retain his position of authority. Psychological studies have shown that people who are most effective, both as parents and as leaders of men, manage to achieve a balance between being kind and friendly and at the same time maintaining their authority. Parents generally keep their authority by asserting their position or by punishing their children from time to time; heads of organisations cannot use quite the same methods, but can employ similar ones, such as maintaining a certain element of formality with their staff.

Achieving a balance between friendliness and maintaining authority means that the head of an organisation should be careful not to swing too much to either extreme. On the one hand he must not carry his friendliness to such lengths that he generates feelings of complete equality, otherwise he will tend to find himself taken for granted and the workforce will take advantage of him. Equally, on the other hand, he must not be too austere and authoritarian, otherwise he will not be able to inspire feelings of affection and loyalty among his staff. It is a judicious blend of friendliness and authority that has to be achieved.

Generally speaking, it is probably true to say that most managers in business err on the side of being too authoritarian and do not show sufficient concern for their employees as human beings. The importance of showing such concern was established in the Hawthorne Works experiments and has now become generally accepted. In the Hawthorne Works the first experiment involved increasing the illumination in one of the workshops, and it was found that output subsequently increased. The investigators then tried decreasing the illumination, expecting to find that output would decrease. But instead, output again increased. This seemed to point to the conclusion that it was not changes in illumination but the concern which the management was apparently showing for the workers which had been responsible for the increases in output, through its effect in increasing the workers' morale.

There are numerous ways in which managers can show that they are concerned about the welfare of their workers, such as by allowing days off for special occasions without too much fuss, generous sick leave payments, providing good cloakroom facilities and so on. But the important thing is that these are symbols of management's concern and will be worth much less if the concern does not get across.

Another important thing for maintaining morale is that the worker should become personally involved in the job. He should be made to feel that the work is important and that what he does counts. One way of accomplishing this is to give the employees a good deal of information about how the company is doing, possibly by making known the profit record each month (as Mr Vinson describes in his account of Plastic Coatings and Mr Dickman in his chapter on Fidelity Radio) or at some other interval. This is also done by profit-sharing schemes. These not only give the workers a direct personal financial interest in increasing the company's profitability, but also involve them psychologically with the company so that they feel they are part of a team who are cooperating together to make the company as a whole operate efficiently. It is this feeling of belonging to a good team that the manager should endeavour to generate.

The entrepreneur has an advantage over the larger companies here because his company is small, and it is easier to generate high morale in a small group than in a big one. There are probably several reasons for this. In a small group everyone knows are another, can work together, generally come to like one another and everyone realises that his own contribution is important. There is an immediate feeling of personal worth and significance. When the group gets too large it is apt to split into little groups which begin to quarrel with one another. Those who have worked in large organisations will know how easy it is for internal feuds to develop between different groups, and these internal wars naturally act to the detriment of the company's efficiency.

Even when the entrepreneur's firm begins to grow it is important to try to keep the work teams fairly small in the interests of maintaining good morale. It has several times been shown that small firms, and small units within firms, have less absenteeism, a lower labour turnover and better productivity records. Mr Nigel Vinson explains how when he expanded Plastic Coatings he took good care to keep the size of the operating units fairly small. It is well known that the best small firms are much more efficient in terms of profit return on capital than the giant companies; they make something of the order of 20 to 30 per cent on capital value, compared with the 5 to 10 per cent which is typical of very large companies. One of the reasons for this is almost certainly that in the smaller firms there is higher morale.

EXPANSION AND DIVERSIFICATION

When the entrepreneur first establishes his business he will have only a small handful of staff. But if things go well he will soon want to expand, and this brings additional problems. One of these is premises. It should be borne in mind that planning regulations are strict and it may be quite difficult to build a factory exactly where one would like it. It may be possible to buy a factory, and a common method of expansion is to buy an existing company together with its premises. Alternatively, it may be necessary to visit the local planning officer to discuss where expansion will be allowed.

At this stage, the entrepreneur who is manufacturing should probably consider producing a different product. Diversification provides an insurance against any sudden collapses in the market which can occur for some reason or another quite beyond the entrepreneur's control. For instance, Mr Dickman of Fidelity Radio tells how the sudden imposition of a high rate of purchase tax on tape recorders reduced his sales by half. Fortunately he had other products —radios and record players—and the continued production of these softened this particular blow of fate. For the entrepreneur in a service industry diversification is less important. Thus Mr Dermot Ryan had built a considerable business in car hire before he diversified into hotels. Mr Raitz has felt sufficiently confident of the continuous expansion of the package holiday industry that he has never diversified at all. Obviously the wisdom of diversification will vary with each particular business. But as a general rule it is probably best to remember the adage that it is unwise to have all your eggs in the same basket.

One of the problems accompanying growth lies in the expansion of management. Hitherto the entrepreneur has probably been the sole manager and has done all the management himself, or perhaps he has had one partner and has shared the management. But with expansion he will begin to take on managers for different functions—for production sales, for new factories in different areas, and so forth. Instead of being the head of a single team, the company comes to consist of a number of teams, each with its own departmental head, and the original entrepreneur is the overall supervisor of all the departmental managers. Many entrepreneurs find this change quite a difficult adjustment to make, because their instinct is to be in the front line where the action is, and now they have to retire from the front line and learn not to interfere in the detailed administration of the different departments. In fact some entrepreneurs who reach this position begin to wonder what exactly their job is. Yet is is important to learn to delegate responsibility if good managers are to be kept. They will want responsibility and authority if they are going to be any good.

But the problem of growing large is a good sort of problem to have. Let us hope, in concluding this introduction, that many readers who take the challenging path of entrepreneurship will eventually encounter them.

2 Hilton Transport Services

RALPH HILTON

I was born and brought up in a working-class family in Deptford in south-east London. I left school at the age of fourteen in the mid-1930s and my first job was as a pageboy at the Hotel Rubens. At that time I can remember thinking that I would not be content to remain a pageboy for long. My ambition then was first to become the hotel's commissionaire and eventually to own my own hotel.

The Second World War played some part in changing this ambition. I served in the army and one of the things I learned was how to service and repair lorries. This knowledge was later to play a decisive part in the development of my transport business. However, it was some years before my interests turned in this direction.

During the war my father ran a pub, and when I was demobbed in 1948 I worked for him. I was still ambitious and fully intended to have a chain of pubs and then hotels of my own. But there was one big problem—I had no money. I approached all the brewers to try to get a pub on tick, and soon got the message: no money, no pub.

I then decided to look around for a sideline, and noticed an advert in the local paper of a haulage business for sale, netting £15 per week clear profit, and only working from 6.30 a.m. to 11.00 a.m. The asking price was £850. Tongue in cheek, I answered the advert. It was then I found that no one could enter the haulage business unless they held an 'A' licence granted by the Ministry of Transport which entitled the holder to carry goods for hire and reward for anyone and anywhere. These licences were virtually impossible to obtain from the MOT, and I mention this here as throughout the story of Hilton Transport Services these licences play a very important part.

As I had no money, I had to persuade the owner of the haulage business to accept deferred terms, without the payment of any deposit. The owner of the business was an elderly gentleman who took a bit of persuading to accept these deferred terms. Why should he trust me, he wanted to know? I was a complete stranger and could offer no security.

To convince him, I said I would be willing to trust him by giving him the £15 profit each week without a receipt, and when he had been paid in full, then he could pass the business to me. This convinced him and he said 'Lad, let's go to a solicitor and get a legal document drawn up'. This was in October 1954. I was thirty-one years old. This was my first business deal and was the birth of Hilton Transport Services. I learnt a lot from that first deal about the advantages of deferred payments which led to the many that followed.

GROWTH OF HILTON TRANSPORT SERVICES

The haulage business I had bought consisted of collecting fish from Billingsgate market and delivering to shops in south-east London areas. The vehicle was a covered van. I drove it myself, and by dashing around like a madman, I managed to reduce the finishing time from 11.00 a.m. to 9.30 a.m. This left a good many free hours during the day. To keep the vehicle occupied and increase my earnings, I approached the local council and asked them to put me on their list as a household removal contractor, and after being accepted, because I was the cheapest, I soon began polishing off two or three household removals a day, after the fish round. I did not go in for classy removals, and I'm afraid many a piano and wardrobe suffered, getting it up and down the stairs; but to compensate for this, I was cheap.

Fish in the mornings and removals in the afternoon was not a good mix. I would hose down the vehicle after the fish and sprinkle it with disinfectant, and when the house owners asked what the fishy smell was, I told them that it came from chemicals that I had been delivering in the mornings.

To keep my father happy, my wife covered my duties of serving in the pub during the day, while I did the heavy work of lifting crates and cleaning etc. during the night. The fish and removal business was so successful that by the end of the year, a matter of only four months, I managed to repay the deferred payments; and being expansion-minded, I purchased another second-hand vehicle. Thus the fleet had doubled by the end of 1954.

With the second vehicle I developed the idea of a hiring removal service by the hour at any time of the day or night. My assistant who had helped with the removals became the full-time driver of the second vehicle. I built up the business by means of adverts I hung up in the pub and by personal calls to all local firms.

Most of the hauliers in the district were only prepared to hire their vehicles for the day, which meant that it was very expensive for anyone who only had work for a vehicle for a couple of hours. The demand for my hourly service caught on so much that I was able to sub-hire vehicles from other hauliers, guaranteeing them a day's work by spreading the time over two or three of my customers who were using the vehicle for a few hours each. As the sub-contracting grew it prompted me to begin purchasing small haulage businesses with 'A' licences, in order that the work could be carried by my own vehicles which was more profitable than subcontracting.

Before proceeding into 1955 I cannot let 1954 go by without mentioning an association that took place, which at that time was not too significant but finally contributed towards the success of Hilton Transport Services. It came about whilst I was delivering fish to one of my clients in Peckham. I vividly remember dashing into the shop and asking the proprietor where was old Wilkie (the previous owner). The proprietor looked up and said that I would never live as long as him by dashing around the way I was. He told me to slow down and have a cup of tea and then as we were talking I told him that I was intending to expand the haulage business. He said that if I was going to, it was essential that I had a good auditor, solicitor and bank manager. Agreeing with the customer that he is always right, I said 'Can you recommend the wise three?' and to my surprise he said 'yes'. The bank manager I wasn't worried about but I was concerned as to where I was going to find the surplus cash for the auditor and solicitor. The client immediately arranged the introductions. Fortunately the auditor and solicitor were two chaps who like me were just beginning their careers and so their fees were very reasonable. I must say that both have been of tremendous help to me.

The introduction to the bank was very profitable. I remember sitting in the bank manager's office in my smelly fishy overalls, saying 'The fried fish shop proprietor has recommended me, and could I please have an overdraft of £300'! I must have looked very pitiful because he said to me 'You look a hard worker' and granted the overdraft, without any security. Or perhaps he wanted me out of his office quickly because of my fishy smell.

In 1955, British Road Services was denationalised and selling vehicles with 'A' licences. At this time getting a licence was more difficult than getting a lorry, and the denationalisation of British Road Services presented a great opportunity. One could tender for these licensed lorries, and if accepted could assign them to a third party for a profit. I was able to obtain three licences and vehicles from the proceeds of such profits. I also purchased three small haulage companies on the deferred terms basis; each had one vehicle, and at the end of 1955 the fleet had grown from two to eight vehicles. The bank overdraft was used for the deposit on these business requisitions and I used hire purchase facilities for the new vehicles I had begun to buy.

At this time I gave up the fish round and house removals, and the business concentrated on the hourly hire which was really going great guns. Although the fleet had increased to eight, with the amount of business flowing in, additional vehicles and 'A' licences were urgently required. My acquisitions for 'A' licences would only take place when I saw that sub-contracting figures were above 20 per cent of my turnover. This was my guideline that it was safe to acquire, as the vehicles purchased were then assured of being fully utilised. Our turnover at the end of 1955 was just under £10,000.

1956 was a prominent landmark for Hilton Transport Services, and a very hectic year. I purchased a petrol filling station, with equipped workshop, and garage space at the rear for all my lorries. This was on the main A3 at Clapham, and was purchased on deferred terms and without a deposit. My main purpose in this acquisition was to house and maintain the haulage vehicles which were, up to then, being worked upon and left in the streets.

Petrol sales and garage repair profits were such that the transport fleet enjoyed free rental and free use of all services, i.e. high pressure lubrication and telescopic lifts, a luxury never before enjoyed. The whole of the garage front was developed to advertise the transport services, as by then I knew, without any shadow of doubt, that transport was to be my exclusive interest and would eventually require my full time.

At the same time as I acquired the filling station, my father decided to retire. I then took over the licence of the pub and landed up, along with my wife, literally running the three businesses—the haulage, the garage and the pub—both of us working morning, noon and night. We decided that this could not continue and planned to phase out the pub first and garage second, over a period of eight years, which was the time I had estimated that the transport business would be really established and on its feet. All three businesses did better than expected and I managed to phase out the pub in three years and the garage two years later, ploughing back the capital profit of each into the transport business.

The transport fleet did not stand still. It increased from eight to sixteen vehicles operating on hourly hire. The cash for this expansion came from the profits being ploughed back, and increased bank and hire purchase facilities. Turnover at the end of 1956 was £18,000.

1957 to 1959 saw the fleet grow from sixteen to forty-nine, operating from depots acquired at Clapham, Greenwich and

Vauxhall. During this period I extended the hourly hire service into the contract hire field, supplying vehicles with drivers on a one- to five-year period, and offering to paint the vehicles in the customer's 'livery' if required. The combined sales for transport and the garage in 1959 had reached £69,000. Administration and accounts staff consisted of my wife, a transport manager and myself, and between us we coped with all correspondence, sales and purchases, day books and ledgers, for the transport, filling station and pub. Needless to say most of this work was carried out last thing at night and at weekends, which certainly kept my wife and me very busy. The nominal and private ledgers were kept and written up by the auditors annually at their offices which, although not to my liking, was the most convenient at the time.

If problems occurred I certainly did not notice them. Indeed I suppose that life was so hectic that I was forced to take decisions as they appeared on the spot and did not have time to find out whether they were right or wrong. As long as sales were increasing in all businesses I was quite content to put up with the day-to-day frustrations and problems, and could always enjoy a good night's sleep.

It was in 1959 that the auditors advised me that in order to reduce my personal risks, and for tax purposes, I should form a limited company. This we did, my wife and I as directors. One wondered at that time where on earth we were going to find the time to hold the board meetings. The only spare time available was just before going to sleep and we both felt so tired, it was easiest to agree and go to sleep. That way there was always perfect harmony on the board.

It was impossible for me to work on budgets, cash flows or forecasts, but as I kept complete control of all purchases, the petty cash, stocks, the bank and hire purchase positions, and balanced the books, using my own methods, I always knew that I was well on the right side. Knowing this position enabled me to sell the pub to give me more time for the transport development, and so ended 1959.

Between 1960 to 1961, the fleet increased to seventy vehicles, partly by purchasing many small hauliers, and also by increasing the contract hire fleet, and spreading the business over a wider area. When purchasing a business, the method I used for valuing was my own assessment of the market value for vehicles, stock and equipment, plus the value of the 'A' licences. I was not interested in their goodwill, and did not pay for any, as, in the main, they were run-down businesses, operating on poor rates. I had built up a surplus of good business, and only needed the vehicles and the 'A' licences.

To assist the acceptance of my offers to purchase on deferred terms, I offered some of the owners a job. They had virtually no alternative but to accept or go bust. Strange as it may seem, many of the owners who had had years of experience and knowledge behind them joined me and have been of valuable assistance. Many of the business owners I have employed are still with us today performing very useful functions and are very happy indeed. It seems, and they admit it themselves, that without the worry of owning their own business, they work better.

At the end of 1961 I sold the filling station, as the cash was required to finance the purchase of a freehold transport depot and warehouse at Croydon. This business consisted of collecting canned goods etc. for the grocery trade, storing, sorting and finally delivering them to retail shops. Small though it was—the warehouse was only 1,500 square feet— I realised the potential of this market. Two local competitors in the area approached me and offered their businesses for sale, both stating that since I had moved into the area they felt that their chances of expanding were virtually nil, which I took as a compliment. Both were acquired and absorbed into the one freehold depot, which proved successful and paved the way for rationalisation by the acquisition of more warehouses.

Hilton Transport Services' inclusive service consisted then of local hire with open and covered vehicles of medium range, contract hire, storage and distribution to the grocery trade in the Croydon area. We were on our way towards offering a comprehensive service to clients. At the year ending 1961 turnover was £134,000, our vehicle strength was seventy and we still relied solely on bank and hire purchase facilities.

Entering into 1962, it was apparent that the business needed help, particularly on the accounting and financial side. I was getting bogged down with too much time being spent in the office. Larger acquisitions and premises were being sought and the bank was requiring up-to-date financial information and accounts. My auditors also realised this and with their help we advertised for an accountant. I can well recall their words, that to find an accountant who would stand the pace I needed would be a miracle. Nevertheless, we did find an accountant who had the necessary qualifications and who was willing to take his coat off and get cracking.

Continuing the history, we are now in the year 1963, and are still looking for acquisitions and extensions into the industry. With the figures and accounts up to date, we were able to prove to the bank our financial stability, and I am glad to say the bank had confidence in us and granted us facilities accordingly. With the help of the bank, and our own resources, between 1962 and 1966 we had acquired additional premises at Thornton Heath, Bermondsey, Eltham, Grays and Streatham, making the total number of depots operating in London eight, together with a total vehicle strength of 347 vehicles by the end of 1966. Turnover in this year was £628,000. Each depot had its own vehicles and a manager who was responsible for their operation and maintenance, and control of drivers and fitters, but who was still under my guidance from head office which was then at Vauxhall. Added to our other services, we had by now extended into the long-distance haulage business and had a wider range of vehicles, i.e. from the smallest to the maximum carrying capacity. We found that by offering our clients such a variety of services we tended to keep competition out.

As we now had eight depots in the London vicinity, each with a full complement of personnel, it was plain to see that another rationalisation scheme was necessary. We began looking for a site with warehouse accommodation with adequate open space to house at least three or four of our existing depots, and large enough to allow for future expansion. Geographically it had to be situated where most of our business lay and near to the major trunk roads. We also had in mind that containerisation was rapidly developing, and therefore we required large enough space to accommodate this business, which we intended to go into.

After extensive searches and enquiries, we found the Charlton site in south-east London. It was an area of 6 acres which suited our requirements admirably. Naturally cash was required and the sum needed was outside the scope of the banks and hire purchase companies. Our auditors introduced us to the Industrial and Commercial Finance Corporation. We were quickly vetted and obtained a loan with which, together with the sale of existing premises, we purchased the Charlton freehold site in 1967 and thus carried out our rationalisation scheme as planned.

The Charlton site was an old glass works, and apart from one good warehouse and plenty of open space, the rest left a lot to be desired. We improvised old buildings for workshops and offices whilst development was going on. Purchasing the site meant that warehousing capacity was increased from 4,500 square feet to 92,000 square feet. I could not afford the time to wait for the warehouses to be filled with business obtained from our sales resources, so I decided to purchase a ready-made business that could fill or at least part fill them immediately. I found a company, Messrs Gayfew Transport Services, who were brimming over with this type of business. They were acquired and transferred lock, stock and barrel to Charlton with their management. They previously had a well-run organisation, even though they were operating from railway arches, and as soon as their business was transferred into our first-class warehouse, their clients increased their throughput with us and, together with our own sales force, within three months of purchasing the Charlton site, all warehouses were full to capacity.

Prior to taking possession of the Charlton site, a management team was being gathered together, and with the purchase of Gayfews I decided that it was time for Hilton Transport Services to end its reign as a one-man band, which had been ably assisted by Mrs Hilton. Mrs Hilton retired

C

and an enlarged board was formed with five directors, myself as managing director. Each director was given responsibility and delegation for his own division, which were warehousing, engineering, finance, sales and traffic.

At the first board meeting of the new directors, it was decided to delete the name of Ralph Hilton from all vehicles and literature. We had a complete change of livery and colours and adopted the letters HTS with the slogan 'Driving force for Industry'.

The Charlton site with its considerable open areas was ideal for storage of containers. Deep-sea containers were in their infancy and we were in on the ground floor. Very few competitors had the space or equipment necessary and we soon became the leaders in this field. By quickly purchasing the correct handling equipment for lifting containers we could offer major shipping lines a container pool facility. This entailed holding stocks of the shipping line containers, having direct contact with their clients for the loading and unloading movements, recording and reporting on the service condition of the containers, and repairing where necessary. The Charlton site afforded us room for opportunities to expand into services allied to our present operations, such as Customs and Excise approved warehouses, shipping and forwarding, tarpaulin manufacturing, insurance and a security force. Each of these divisions was set up by the management that had previously been assembled, with the instructions that they must not rely solely on HTS but go out on their own and get business. Today all these divisions are doing very well and contribute to the Group's profit.

1968 did not go by without the average percentage of acquisitions, and at the end of the year the fleet totalled over 400 vehicles and the turnover was £1,126,000.

1969 began with a merger, all in shares, with our nearest competitor, Messrs William Joy, who were situated only a matter of yards from our Charlton depot. This was a company that had had a similar background to that of HTS, commencing more or less at the same time (1954) from a one-vehicle outfit, which had built up to a 140-vehicle fleet, and 21,000 square feet of warehousing on valuable freehold property. The business conducted by them was exactly the same as ours, with the same type of vehicles and, most important of all, similarly progressive management. The whole team joined us, and from the word go it was an immediate success. With the merger, rationalisation of depots and management was again put in hand and provided tremendous savings.

By this time we had attracted transport and warehouse business from virtually all the big household names in the UK. Many were asking for our services in the provinces, in particular in Manchester and Southampton. We therefore looked for suitable acquisitions in these areas and were fortunate to find one company which was operating in both towns. The company, W. Reeves & Sons Ltd, had been founded and built by Mr Reeves in a matter of ten years. They also were progressive, not afraid of hard work and spoke our language. This was another natural merger, again by shares, and Mr Reeves joined our main board.

The effects of the merger were twofold in that Reeves were looking for work to complete their triangular movements. They had work from Manchester to Southampton and Southampton to London, but were weak on traffic from London to Manchester. We supplied this and at the same time gained the two important depots, where we had business waiting to operate from.

I had always envisaged that what we had achieved in London could be achieved nationally. I mean the rationalisation which followed acquisitions and the merging of businesses. This was now taking place throughout the UK and as a result, early in 1970, businesses were acquired at Newcastle, Liverpool and Gloucester, and in these instances for cash on the nail, something unusual for HTS.

The business prospered mainly because we could offer clients a package deal price for collecting from factory production floor, transporting, holding stocks in warehouses and effecting final delivery to retail outlets against their salesmen's orders. This comprehensive service forced us to increase our warehousing facilities and we purchased an adjoining site of 4 acres at Charlton which had an old warehouse of 100,000 square feet on the site. To finance this, ICFC came to our aid for the second time. We had informed them at our first meeting that we would be back and that within a short time we would be back yet again. After a while the old warehouse became too costly to operate as it was of the double storey type and had many obstructing pillars. As we were now the owners of a 10-acre site, it was felt that it was well worth while developing it for the future. We went back to ICFC for the third time and asked for £600,000 for the building costs. This loan was agreed. We put the building of the warehouses in hand, and even before they were completed we had obtained business waiting to go in. In fact, as soon as the builders put the roof on, and after they had sectioned it off, we moved in. This meant that we were earning profits before the buildings were paid for. All warehouses are now working to full capacity.

Good fortune fell HTS's way in June of 1970. Our neighbours Messrs G. A. Harvey who owned a 180,000 square feet engineering building decided to sell. We looked at the building and found it was ideal for our container operation, due to its height. It was also ideal in that it was equipped with eight 40-ton capacity overhead travelling cranes, which meant that loaded containers could be stacked three high and block stowed. With these craneage facilities we could also enter the heavy lift business and storage of machinery etc. As with the distribution and warehousing these heavy lift services, introduced to the transport and other divisions of the group, gave outlets to additional business. The Harvey building was purchased freehold and payments were deferred and spread over a five-year term.

FORMATION OF THE PUBLIC COMPANY IN 1970

We were now short of cash. This was inevitable after acquiring various premises and businesses for cash and having to make the initial payment for the Harvey building, together with the need for a far larger working capital to cope with the increased business. To bring in more funds we decided to go public. This happened in November 1970. The funds raised from public subscription, together with the cash we had received from the sale of equity to ICFC, gave us £830,000 for ploughing back into the company.

We were very relieved when this operation was over. Months of preparation had taken place, independent auditors and our own auditors were extracting information from all personnel, which was very time-consuming, to say nothing of the prospectus meetings, at which slide-rules got hot from being overworked. I felt that the time spent on these probably cost us six good acquisitions.

With the flotation over, we settled down to putting our plan of developing a complete freight complex throughout the UK into operation. If any item needs to be moved, large or small, either by rail, road, sea or air, and may require other services such as warehousing en route, packing or unpacking, special documentation, such as Customs and Excise procedures, we are prepared to do the job.

We are well on the way to achieving this in the UK and are now making headway into Europe. The European traffic will be considerably enhanced by the granting of the Customs and Excise approval on part of our Charlton site. Clients can, for example, purchase say 500 tons of goods from anywhere on the Continent and require them to be distributed to outlets in small consignments in the UK, possibly over a period of time and also in rotation. All they need to do is contact us and we can arrange the whole operation, supplying all services other than ships and labour at the ports. The Customs and Excise approval took four years to obtain. We applied for it when we first acquired the Charlton site which shows that we were thinking ahead.

The Common Market presents further opportunity for our business. We are at present actively engaged in hauling to and from the Continent, but are restricted by Government permits for the number of movements and destinations. These permits do not apply to the hauliers of Common Market countries; they are free to go where they like and no doubt the restrictions on us will be lifted if and when we enter the community, giving us freedom of movement.

Although we are transporting goods overseas by container

and trailer there is still a large proportion of business that has to be packed and crated, i.e. the export packing business. The packing business blends quite well with our operation, so it was inevitable that a packing company should be purchased. One was found, purchased by shares and merged, and the packing services now extend to main depots.

THE PRESENT POSITION OF HILTON TRANSPORT SERVICES

As a freight complex we are now probably the third largest in the UK, the largest being the British Road Services and the second largest the Transport and Development Group. Our company has about one per cent of the market. Looking back, it is a coincidence that it was the BRS that helped us in the early stages when we obtained those valuable 'A' licences from them in 1955. 'A' licences were abolished in 1968 and were replaced by 'O' licences. This type of licence protects the industry even more than before, as these are only granted to people who can satisfy the Ministry of Transport that vehicles have adequate garage facilities, are maintained correctly and regularly, and that the company have the necessary professional operational staff and are of sound financial structure. If this law had been in force in 1954 I would not be writing about a freight complex. Perhaps I might have been able to persuade a brewer to give me a pub on deferred terms and be writing about the alcohol business instead.

MANAGEMENT

The team began back in 1954, indeed from my very first employee and from those who joined me in the early days. For the first ten years I interviewed virtually every new employee myself, and if they were suitable I told them that providing they were prepared to give me their loyalty and were not afraid of hard work they would not look back. As a result of this two of the early employees are on the main board, and many more are depot managers, transport managers and so forth. All have risen from the ranks. Eight out of the first ten employees are still with the company today.

The qualifications I look for in a person are loyalty, honesty and the giving of his best. Even though his best may not be of directorship material, there are many important positions for loyal servants to fill. To give an example, my first employee unfortunately has not the ability to become a depot manager or even a transport manager, but I could trust him with a million pounds, so I gave him the chief cashier's job. His salary is more or less in line with that of a director, which may sound expensive for a cashier but it is worth every penny. He is even more close fisted than I am when it comes to paying out cash.

I find that for the operational managerial positions, by far the best are those that have risen from the ranks: they have the practical knowledge of what is required, and are well versed in all the dodges that drivers and others get up to —and there are many, such as where a driver, having finished his day's work, would ring in to say he had just finished his last delivery, say in Oxford, and would be back to the depot three hours later. If the traffic manager is on the ball he will ask the driver what number he is ringing from only to find that he is calling from home. Another is to cure drivers of persistently asking the manager for beer money jobs. I remember even just recently a manager telling a driver that he was putting him on a job the next day where he was to be particularly careful as he was to carry passengers. After the driver had gone I immediately started to tell the manager of the rule that they must not let a driver know what job he was going on the next day, to which he quickly remarked, he'll get no beer money from these passengers, they are all stiff—the job is to move coffins from one cemetery to another. That will cure him of asking for beer money jobs. Firmness of this kind leads to a manager being respected.

It is human nature that manual workers will do more than their day's work providing they get rewarded. This we do not mind providing the company gets its share. Incentive schemes for manual workers are in force, some based on sharing part of the revenue over certain targets, others by quality and performance of work. This has the effect that most of the manual workers govern their own destiny as far as wages are concerned and it makes them individualists. It is also assists in avoiding any union unrest that could otherwise arise. Our workers are union members but it is accepted that they have to be in order to be able to carry out their work, i.e. at the docks and strong union concerns. Due to these incentive schemes, and the respect in which the managers are held, we enjoy good labour relations. Staff personnel do not have incentive schemes but are paid above the average salaries. Their chances of promotion are very good and this keeps them keen and ambitious.

The provincial depots receive the same treatment as the depot in London. The directors of the company make regular visits. The drivers from the provincial depots regularly call into London in the execution of their duties and therefore feel equally part of the team.

Meetings are encouraged amongst department managers so that they get to know each other's problems. Such is the keeness that most of these meetings take place after normal hours but this is left entirely to their own discretion. My motto has always been 'Do not be critical against another department, go find the problems that face them'. These get-togethers have helped considerably in this respect. All directors have lunch together on the premises and one can say that a board meeting is held every day. With the discussions that take place at the working lunches we all know what's happening and prepare and plan for improvements on what is taking place and the future.

When acquisitions are made, one of the first tasks is to acquaint all workers of the new company who we are, how we go about things, what is expected of them and to reassure them of their security. We recognise that our business depends materially on service and is passed on by those who contact the customers, mainly the drivers.

FINANCIAL

From its inception the business was purchased on deferred

payments, without deposit, which was a method adopted throughout virtually all acquisitions up to 1968. When I first began with one vehicle, capital was not an immediate headache, as driving myself, without drawing wages or stamps (these coming from the pub), meant that after paying the running costs and a contingency for replacement of vehicle all the balance was paid to the vendor. Although I had planned that it would take nine months to complete the deferred payments of purchase, by obtaining the maximum use of the vehicle and substantially increasing the runover as compared with the previous owner, I was able to complete the transaction in three months. The cost of this transaction was £850 inclusive of interest, the largest asset being the 'A' licence then valued at £500, the vehicle and the goodwill together representing £350.

Briefly, an 'A' licence issued by the Ministry of Transport authorises the holder to carry, within reason, any goods, for anyone, anywhere. 'B' and 'C' licences were also issued by the Ministry of Transport, the former permitting only certain named goods or clients for hire and reward and restricted to certain areas, and the latter used only for users and manufactures carrying their own goods. To obtain these 'A' and 'B' licences, the easiest and quickest method was by purchasing those issued to other transport businesses but this of course was the most expensive. One could also apply to the Ministry of Transport, but it was virtually impossible to get an 'A' licence and only marginally less to obtain a 'B'; the applications were extremely time-consuming and uncertain, but if successful were much cheaper than purchasing. The 'A' ,'B' and 'C' licensing was abolished in 1968–9 by the introduction of the 'O' licence, issued quite freely by the Ministry of Transport providing satisfactory maintenance, technical and operational ability can be proved. This licensing position has been explained because (a) acquisitions for 1954 to 1968 were to obtain the 'A' and 'B' licences only and (b) it was difficult to raise cash for these as there was no security value whatsoever to a lender.

Returning to the completed purchase of our first vehicle with the 'A' licence in 1954, I made the first of many applications for an 'A' licence. Strange as it may seem, of the many applications made to the Ministry of Transport for additional licences the only two that were successful were the one for the vehicle I immediately applied for at the end of the first three months in business, the other for a block of six some years later. This early piece of luck meant that I was able to double the fleet at that time by purchasing a cheap second-hand vehicle outright, without the expense of finding cash for the licence. This was vitally important at that stage, affording me the chance to build a healthy balance sheet showing good profits. Overheads were very low, since I continued to drive, maintain and repair the two vehicles, look after the accounts, had only one employee, and was still drawing a salary from my father's pub and ploughing back all profits.

With the healthy balance sheet the Westminster Bank, whom I had contacted for the first time, even then with un-audited accounts, granted an overdraft facility of £300. I then embarked on acquiring one or two vehicle transport concerns for their licences, putting down a deposit and the balance on deferred terms. I then began replacing the vehicles which in the main were petrol driven with new diesel vehicles, using the facilities of hire purchase spread over two years. Simple arithmetic proved that replacing petrol vehicles with an MPG of 7 to 8 with diesel vehicles with an MPG of 20 to 24 gave considerable savings on fuel costs which paid the hire purchase repayments.

Larger vehicle transport businesses with premises were then being acquired. As each was added the overdraft and loan from the bank grew larger and likewise the hire purchase. By 1960 the overdraft was around £30,000, the hire purchase commitment more or less the same. As each request to the bank was made many hours were spent in negotiation, and tribute must be paid to the valuable advice of the two bank managers of the local branch who, apart from arranging the advances, were extremely helpful in guiding me to keep within budgets and costs and improve my credit control, and in general took an interest in the business, to me a first-class free service. I was also helped by some of the hire purchase companies which made me personal loans which were put into the business. By 1966 the overdraft facility was just over £100,000 but the company was seeking cash outside the bank's line of business, i.e. large warehouse premises to consolidate, and in the search for this cash the most important factor to the company was the ICFC. A proposition was put to them for the purchase of a 6-acre site, and in a businesslike manner, within a matter of just a few days, the answer in principle was 'yes', for nearly £250,000. We quickly realised the value of the name of ICFC. Even though it was not an equity holder, the truth soon became apparent of the stock phrase I have heard from many financial people, 'if the ICFC have vetted you and loaned, its good enough for us', and cash was being offered from many other sources but never taken up. The other advantage which was of considerable help was the personal contact between the ICFC and our clearing bank which meant that on many an occasion, just by telephone, the bank would 'bridge' whilst ICFC were preparing documents for solicitors which obviously took some time and in some cases months. It was clear that the Charlton site was a launching pad for bigger things to come. We saw that to round the site for a good development we needed the adjoining 4 acres. Again a trip was made to ICFC who promptly answered our request with a further £160,000 to purchase the site, giving a polite warning that the next time a loan was sought, equity would be required. Needless to add, having acquired the 10-acre site, development of warehouses and workshops were essential and obviously this required more capital. We went again to ICFC and in this instance we agreed to sell 15 per cent of our equity for £240,000 plus the additional raising of a further loan of £290,000, and so the development was financed.

Even before the warehouses were built they were virtually full with business waiting to come in. Within a matter of months of completion of the new buildings, by our good fortune our adjoining neighbour, G. A. Harvey, was running into heavy losses in operating a very large engineering shop of nearly 200,000 square feet and therefore decided to close down and sell the premises. This particular building suited our needs, especially for the handling of containers as there were eight overhead 40-ton travelling cranes already installed and as it was adjacent to our existing 10 acres we could not afford to lose the opportunity of purchasing freehold. We were fortunate to obtain the building for the sum of £474,000 on deferred terms but only for a period of five years. To raise the necessary instalments, to improve our cash flow—always a problem due to our very rapid expansion—and to reduce our bank overdraft, which by then was in the region of £350,000, we decided to make a public flotation of the company. This was successfully handled by ICFC and the company benefited by over £600,000 from the issue.

Hardly had the ink dried on the flotation contracts when the company, looking for further expansion, made a bid for another floated transport company by shares and cash. The ICFC negotiated all dealings on our behalf including the placings of our shares that were necessary.

Summing up the financial affairs, excluding all accountancy work, the company was able to expand rapidly using methods of (*a*) deferred payments when acquiring businesses, (*b*) facilities and services from the clearing banks, (*c*) taking best advantage of hire purchase facilities, (*d*) vitally important cash flow improved considerably on taking advantages of the tax losses of many of the companies acquired (although not acquired mainly for that reason but to obtain 'A' licences) and (*e*) our association with ICFC and their confidence in our ability to operate a large, successful and efficient comprehensive transport and warehousing organisation.

ACCOUNTING AND FINANCIAL CONTROL

I did the accounts myself from 1954 until 1962 and our accountancy methods during this period were rather rough and ready. In 1962 we took on an accountant, and two girls, and he has introduced a much greater degree of sophistication into our procedures.

All means at the company's disposal had to be marshalled

in the effort to obtain working capital for businesses newly taken over, to cover in some cases deposits or purchase prices agreed to, or businesses and subsequent instalments paid with deferred terms, and for stamp duty and legal costs etc. Our methods of financial control included strict central control of all expenditure, and central control of bulk discounts and credit periods negotiated. We began to supply the bank with up-to-date figures of debtors, sales profits and balance sheets in order to obtain the maximum overdraft facilities. Hitherto, whilst the bank had been good to Hilton Transport Services, the overdraft was 25 per cent of revenue which was about three times the amount normally allowed today and the information the bank required came very slowly from the auditors.

Our accountant then introduced forecasts of monthly revenue, cash flow and profits. This information was invaluable in keeping both the bank and management informed. Provided the purchase price of an acquisition was backed by assets, the bank was usually prepared to offer facilities if shown by the cash flow forecast that they were needed for a temporary period.

We used hire purchase to the limit with several companies. By using more than one company, more competitive rates could be achieved, and by receiving a separate credit line from each it was possible to receive a total credit line exceeding that offered by any one hire purchase company.

By using these methods and by ploughing back all the profits of each year, together with the advantages of having small tax bills due to large capital allowances and losses of acquisitions, we were able to take over sixteen companies between 1962 and 1967. By 1970 a further eighteen companies had been acquired and two additional companies had been formed for insurance brokerage and manufacture of tarpaulins, sheets and ropes.

In 1962 each depot was a separate trading entity running under its previous trading name. This enabled us, with inter-depot trading, to control the profitability of each unit. Early in 1967 a group of three companies involved in storage and distribution was taken over and a separate warehousing division for accounting purposes was created in order that the profitability could be compared with transport. We discovered that storage and distribution, using one's own transport for the distribution, was showing a better return than transport alone. Storage and distribution were complementary to each other, and hence we developed our concentration on storage and distribution when we consolidated our business at Charlton.

Our first approach for finance was made to the ICFC to assist in the purchase of the 6-acre site at Charlton. We were granted 70 per cent of the cost on a twenty-year mortgage after a thorough investigation by ICFC into our business. We realised that whilst the security angle was satisfactory the additional criterion required by ICFC was that the business had to be progressive and well managed. Our public flotation in 1970 has been an advantage in so far as we are now in a position to use our paper for acquisitions instead of the ever useful cash. Recently we acquired a private company costing £130,000 for a nominal share value of £20,000.

Now that we are a rather spread company by location and business, strict control is essential if the best results are to be obtained. The system of control currently in force is that by Tuesday of the following week the details of revenue and cost of every vehicle operated is received at head office in order that under-utilised vehicles can be transferred where necessary to another depot. The various divisions and depots are controlled by the production of monthly consolidated profit and loss accounts, and separate monthly vehicle profit and loss accounts showing individual vehicle costings. All purchases and discounts are negotiated centrally and cover such items as fuel, oil, spares, tyres, insurances etc. In addition, each division or depot, and every individual vehicle, has monthly or weekly targets covering profit, revenue and expenditure.

At present we obtain funds for our development working capital from the bank—our overdraft facility is down to 6 per cent of annual revenue and is normally sufficient to cover our fluctuating requirements of working capital, and for new acquisitions. If additional funds are required for deposits on new vehicles or new premises then temporary arrangements are made with the bank. Vehicles are financed by hire purchase in the main, and due to our large bulk requirement, the rate is very competitive.

Cash profit forecasting is especially important to HTS because of its progression and on these figures is based our long-term policy twelve months ahead. These figures are up-dated at three-months intervals or when acquisitions take place.

POSITION OF HTS IN 1970

The company at present owns and operates over 1,000 vehicles ranging up to 32 tons gross, and 350 heavy duty trailers, engaged principally in short haulage. About 200 of the vehicles are hired out on contract without drivers. The company has warehousing accommodation of some 390,000 square feet in use or under construction, equipped with modern handling equipment for containerisation and distribution. There are over 1,500 customers, including many with household names, spread over a wide variety of industries.

In addition to our headquarters at Charlton, where we have a 26-acre site, we now have warehouses and depots at

Table 2.1   Growth of Turnover and Profit, 1961–70

Years to 31 July:	Turnover £	Profit before taxation £
1961	212,000	21,000
1962	233,000	24,000
1963	281,000	26,000
1964	482,000	46,000
1965	606,000	70,000
1966	831,000	88,000
1967	954,000	89,000
1968	1,422,000	115,000
1969	1,883,000	212,000
1970	2,803,000	319,000

Greenwich, Croydon, Clapham, Streatham, Bermondsey and Thornton Heath in the London area, and also at Manchester, Southampton, Gateshead and Liverpool. Our policy is to set up depots about 100 miles from each other to develop the warehouse and short-haul transport business with the aim of achieving national coverage.

The growth of the company's turnover and profit from 1961 to 1970 is shown in Table 2.1.

3 Land Pyrometers

T. LAND

The idea of Land Pyrometers was born in the wartime black-out on the top deck of a Sheffield tram. At that time, I was developing a new design of liquid steel pyrometer, and if a furnace was melting late in the evening, I had to stay late for my trials. Clanging and clattering homewards in the darkness I had time to think.

On that particular evening the trials must have gone well. We were working to perfect a pyrometer with which the furnaceman could quickly make a reliable measurement of the temperature of the liquid steel in the melting furnace. The principle of the method had been worked out at the National Physical Laboratory. We were converting it into a practical workshop tool. By that time, it was clear that we should succeed, and that the new technique would in due course be adopted by the steel industry throughout the world.

It occurred to me on that journey home that the new technique needed commercial development. People used to visit the steelworks where I was working to see the new pyrometers that I had designed, and I used to make one or two for them in the laboratory to get them started. I did a few sums in my head and I realised that some day before long the British steel industry would be making hundreds of thousands of temperature measurements every year. Every time a measurement was made, a new silica protection tube was fitted over the platinum thermocouple before dipping it for a few seconds into the liquid metal. The tubes cost a shilling each. What with thermocouples and replacement parts, there was going to be a nice little business for some-

D

body. Wouldn't it be interesting to form a company to make liquid steel pyrometers to exploit the new 'quick immersion' technique and spread its use throughout the world! I even gave the company a name—Quick Immersion Ltd. But it was wartime. Young scientists had to get on with winning the war. So the idea remained a daydream until the war ended.

At the end of the war there was a chance to sit back and think about my career. After going to Chesterfield Grammar School and Cambridge University, I had spent a few years in the family business of T. Land & Son Ltd, manufacturers of electroplate and pewter. I had to decide whether to go back to the family business (I was the fourth generation) or continue with my scientific career. I had just been given the job of designing a gas turbine (like a small-scale jet engine) suitable to power a motor bus. It was a fascinating project and my initial decision was to go ahead with scientific research. But I was aware that my parents and the other older members of the Land family depended on the family business, which was in poor shape after the war. The business was my inheritance and my responsibility. Perhaps I could take the remnants of the old company, and on its ruins build the foundations of something new that would combine my scientific and business interests and be my own creation. I hesitated for some months and finally decided to try the new venture.

The classical entrepreneur starts his business with £100 and a second-hand furniture van in a tumbledown garage. We had a relatively comfortable take-off. We had a small existing business, a small factory of our own and perhaps £10,000 working capital. But the existing business was only producing enough income for the older members of the family to live on, and the new business had to create its own working capital as it went along.

Business is founded on knowledge. Ours is founded on the technical knowledge that I had acquired while working for four years as head of the pyrometry department of a Sheffield steelworks. It is a sobering thought that today, twenty-five year later, as much as 95 per cent of the company's sales are in thermocouples and equipment for use in liquid steel and in radiation pyrometers. I acquired my initial experience in all these fields during those four short years.

I returned to the family business in 1947. The old business was enjoying a brief post-war boom. We had a few years to build something new and we had to move quickly. I knew that there was a market for the wires, insulators and protection sheaths that the steelworks use to repair their thermocouples. We could buy them from the manufacturers in bulk on a resale discount and sell them to the pyrometry departments at a reasonable profit. So we engaged a salesman, had him briefly trained at a steelworks, and ordered some stock to sell. We were in business, and in the first year's trading the sales of the pyrometer department were almost equal to the sales of electroplate and pewter. At first we ran both sections under the name of T. Land & Son Ltd, but in 1950 Land Pyrometers Ltd was formed and the old company was sold in 1953.

We shall meet certain technical words and phrases throughout this chapter. It may be helpful to give a brief outline of the technical side of the company's activities, which are not really particularly obscure.

Our business is primarily in industrial temperature measurement. A pyrometer is simply a thermometer by another name; not the mercury-in-glass type that the doctor slips under your tongue or that hangs outside the window, but an electrical thermometer. The word pyrometer is derived from the Greek word for fire, and it is usually applied to a thermometer designed to measure high temperatures.

Pyrometers are of two main types, thermocouples and radiation pyrometers. A thermocouple consists of two wires of different metals, usually laid side by side and kept apart by twin-hole ceramic insulating beads. The wires are welded together at one end. When the junction of the wires is heated, a small voltage is generated at the other end, that can be measured by a meter marked in temperature.

A radiation pyrometer is first cousin to a photographic exposure meter. It measures the temperature of a red hot body by measuring the brightness of the red hot surface. Even if the body is not red hot, the pyrometer can be designed to measure the radiant heat (or 'infra-red radiation') that is emitted instead of the light. The most important feature of a radiation pyrometer is that it measures temperature from a distance without touching the hot body. It can be used to measure the temperature of a red-hot bar of steel as it is being rolled, or a hot sheet of window glass that would crack if it were touched.

GROWTH OF THE COMPANY, 1947–57

We did not have much capital. The old business had an old but serviceable press, a couple of drop-stamps and some polishing lathes. We had perhaps £10,000 of working capital, and we had a small factory, built in 1907, of 10,000 square feet on four flours. We needed to mobilise our resources and set them to work. As the business grew, so did the over-draft—to the great anxiety of my father and my uncle.

After a couple of years my cousin, Eric Land, joined the firm. Although he was only in his early twenties, he seemed to have an aptitude for business and he soon took over the running of the old business while I paid more attention to the new one. Eric is now joint managing director with me and runs much of the day-to-day business of the company, as we shall see later in the story.

As the business quickly grew, and the overdraft grew with it, I soon took a look at the financial needs of the growing business and did a bit of long-term planning on the back of an envelope. We had to generate our own capital and the needs of the older generation took a fair slice out of the modest profits. But I reckoned that we could afford to grow to the point of doing a turnover of £100,000 within ten years. At the time this looked to me to be a rather ambitious plan. In fact we exceeded that figure in the fifth year and reached £200,000 in the ninth year. So we had problems.

We closed down the electroplate business in 1953 but still the business grew. We had to decide in 1957 whether to risk curtailing the growth or risk borrowing some money from

ICFC. It was by a vote of 3 to 2 that the board decided to borrow £20,000 at the rather frightening rate of $7\frac{1}{2}$ per cent per annum.

We now decided that we must prepare ourselves for the further growth that lay ahead. We had added a manufacturing section to the business. I now thought that we would need to build up a network of local offices in the way that other instrument companies did, and we made a start with an office in London. We engaged a buyer to look after the stores which were getting a bit chaotic, and we set up a costing department to keep an eye on the manufacturing costs. The sales office was enlarged and we began to put in systems.

What we did not realise was that we had then got half the market for the thermocouples and thermocouple spares that we were selling, and that the volume of our sales of such items was not going to increase any faster than the growth of steel production for the next fifteen years.

DIFFICULTIES OF 1957–8

The years 1957–8 saw the first post-war recession in the steel industry. Our sales, instead of continuing to rise, first levelled off and then disastrously declined. The sales declined much more than steel production and the profits nearly vanished. We increased the sales force but only sold less. Something serious had gone wrong. We had in fact come to the end of the first phase of the company's growth and we had to think out our business afresh.

There was a profound conflict of opinion on how to get out of our difficulties. Our sales director was in favour of 'accelerating out of the skid'. Eric, who was in charge of production, rightly condemned the overgrown superstructure we had created for future growth. We looked at the simple organisation of our principle competitor who was making a very nice profit. We had the sales volume and we could make a good profit as we had done before but we needed to cut a minimum of £10,000 off the salaries and expenses. This meant some very painful surgery.

It was time to stop thinking about the great company that we were going to become. We concentrated our minds instead on the fact that we were a small company and decided to make the most of the advantages that a small company enjoys. We would simplify our structure and our procedures and shorten our lines of communication to the customer so that he could speak to the man who knew the answers.

We decided that we did not need a sales director. I would take charge of sales myself. We closed the London office, dispensed with a buyer, reduced the sales office drastically and cut the cost office to one girl. One of the three outside salesmen left us immediately and within a year we lost the other two as well.

We waited to see what would happen. Would the tree survive the drastic pruning or would it die? We soon knew the answer. In the next two years the sales increased by 75 per cent, the profits rose to three times the previous record, and the net worth of the company increased by 70 per cent. We were once more a healthy company, indeed a much healthier company than we had ever been before.

During this period the men who were to take the company forward came to the front. It became evident during the crisis that Eric and I held the real power in the company, that we had very different, complementary abilities, and that we could and would work together successfully. Fred Campbell emerged as a man who got results in the stores and the sales office and went on to be sales manager and a director of the company. Bill Longley, who had been engaged as a capstan lathe operator, turned out to know how to run a machine shop and is now production manager.

The immediate effect of the reorganisation in 1959 was to make the company profitable and healthy, and to restore the sales of thermocouples and spares to their previous share of the market. However, we accepted that beyond this point the return on extra sales effort in this field would be small. We contented ourselves for the next seven years with a modest growth and a very modest sales expenditure of between 2 and 3 per cent of the turnover. We concentrated on two objectives. First, we built up the financial resources of the company, and second, we invested as much as we could in the development of our range of radiation pyrometers.

Between 1959 and 1966 the net worth of the company grew from £45,000 to £208,000 and we were able to pay off most of the ICFC loan and build and pay for a new factory with twice the floor area of the old one.

RADIATION PYROMETERS

During this quieter period, we were not inactive. In 1950 we engaged Roy Barber, a young physicist who had worked with me in the steelworks and who is now our technical director. Together we began to develop some ideas that we had begun to explore in our earlier steelworks days. First we developed an idea that I had patented for a pyrometer to measure surface temperature accurately; we then moved on to other types of radiation pyrometer that were in demand.

The instrument firm of George Kent Ltd asked us to develop for them a general purpose radiation pyrometer. Pilkington Brothers asked us to develop a pyrometer to measure the temperature of glass. The National Physical Laboratory taught us how to make the sensitive radiation detectors that they had made during the war. We pioneered the use of silicon solar cells (used to charge the batteries of space vehicles) in radiation pyrometers. We thoroughly enjoyed ourselves and we spent twice as much on research as we devoted to sales.

Slowly and steadily we built a new and profitable product line which today contributes nearly as much to the profits of the company as the thermocouples and spares. More than half these radiation pyrometers are exported.

DISPOSABLE DEVICES FOR LIQUID STEEL

Our early sales had been given a big impetus by the sale of replacement parts—thermocouple wires, insulators and silica sheaths—for liquid steel thermocouples. In the early 1960s the Americans took the original British invention, which they had adopted, and modified it radically. They produced a disposable unit, mounted at the end of a cardboard tube, which was dipped in the liquid steel once and then thrown away. The disposable units were rather expensive but the method was so simple and reliable that it soon displaced the old methods.

The American instrument company that held the patents had a British subsidiary which successfully introduced the new method to the British steel industry. This was a product which we too would have liked to make, but the British patent was very strong and we had to wait on the sidelines. However, a second American company, which had been involved in the development of the new thermocouple from an early date, challenged the American patent and obtained licences both for America and for the UK. We were approached by them and offered the British rights which, after the conclusion of the patent litigation in America, we were delighted to accept.

The new product was launched in 1966 and was an immediate success. We appointed Fred Campbell as sales manager and stepped up the sales effort, introducing an incentive scheme linked to sales of the new disposable thermocouple. The sales continued to grow and we now have a good share of the market. We are following up this success by developing new disposable devices for use in liquid steel. The new steel-making processes that are now replacing the old methods are so fast that new methods of process control are needed, which will involve various new products that we can make. The first of them are just coming on the market.

OVERSEAS COMPANIES

We think that these new products will give us the opportunity that we have been looking for to get into the Common Market countries in a big way. To take advantage of this opportunity we formed a company called S. A. Land Europe N.V. in Belgium in 1970. It will be no easy task to get into the European market and we shall have to pay a heavy 'entrance fee' in the shape of early losses and massive support from the UK. If we can get the new offshoot firmly established we intend to put a big effort into making it grow. The target that we have in mind is to make the European company larger than the UK company within ten years. This target could look very silly in a few years hence, but it is well worth while to make an effort compatible with the size of the European market.

As soon as we had formed Land Europe, we found that the American company that had been distributing our radiation pyrometers in the United States was in financial difficulties. To save our business in the American market, we had to act quickly. We therefore formed a company, Land Instruments Inc., in Tullytown, Pennsylvania, later in 1970. We have enough sales in America to support the company and a good man who knows our products. We do not expect too many problems there, but we could have done very well without two new subsidiaries starting up at the same time!

THE UPS AND DOWNS OF THE STEEL INDUSTRY

We still depend to a large extent on our sales to the steel industry. Unfortunately steel is a cyclic industry that is profoundly affected by the business cycle. We have seen how the steel depression of 1958 affected the company. The effect was dramatic, but in the long run it was healthy. The recessions of 1962 and 1966–7 were relatively mild and new products were available at the right times to cushion the shock. At the time of writing, the steel industry is once again suffering a long and deep recession comparable to the recession of 1958. This time our new products were not quite ready at the lucky moment. So once again there is an anxious period as we wait for steel to revive. This time the company is in good shape and there is no prospect of desperate surgery. But again the effect is proving to be salutary, causing us to re-cast our organisation, review our costs and prices and look more keenly than ever for new markets and new opportunities to turn our knowledge into profitable business.

MANAGING THE BUSINESS

The structure

The management of a business has three aspects. First there is the management structure—who does what and who reports to whom. Secondly there is the system of measurements that is set up to indicate what is happening in the business. Finally there is the operation of the system, the policy one pursues and the means one employs, the principles on which one operates.

My cousin, Eric Land, and I act as joint managing directors. Eric is the organiser, the man who creates the systems and keeps them running smoothly. My interests and aptitudes are more in the entrepreneurial and technical aspects of the business. Our complementary abilities enable us to work together smoothly and effectively.

The form of the organisation has changed as the company has grown. Other companies may operate according to an elegant organisation chart; ours never seems to be operating in quite the classical form. Always the theoretical ideal is distorted by the strengths and weaknesses of the individuals that occupy the boxes on the chart and by the changing needs of the company.

At the time of writing we have recently adopted a divisional structure, dividing the company into two divisions. We did this because we realised that we were neglecting a part of the business that has considerable potential. Our principal sales go into the steel industry. We have built up a sales organisation chiefly from men with experience in the instrument departments of various steel companies. These men know their market intimately and do a wonderful job.

But we have a second part of the business comprising radiation pyrometers and instruments for the fuel technologist. These instruments certainly sell to the steel industry, but they sell in much greater numbers into a much wider market—power stations, glass works, paper mills, carpet manufacturers and all sorts of industries. For all we know the real future of the company may lie in this part of our business.

For this reason my cousin and I have each taken one

division, and we are giving each division our concentrated attention. We each have our own sales force, but the two forces work closely together. The European subsidiary is selling so far only into the steel industry, and is therefore made responsible to Eric and his metal industries division. The American company sells radiation pyrometers and is my responsibility.

Product development is the responsibility of the technical director, who is in charge of technical development in both divisions. Eric and I each have access to the development people working for our divisions. Together we decide on the allocation of resources between divisions. We each have our assembly departments, but we make use of a single machine shop that makes components for both divisions.

The present organisation has the look of a temporary expedient designed to meet the challenge of the present trade recession. We have split the company in such a way that it can be run as two small businesses, each given personal, concentrated attention by one managing director. This is highly effective at this stage in the company's development. It may be quite inappropriate in five years' time.

The system of measurements

The management accounts form an integral part of the accounting system. They incorporate a system of budgetary control and we produce every quarter a trading account, a balance sheet and a sales analysis, and once a year a company profit statement and a contribution statement. The accounts also include a system of responsibility accounting which provides quarterly statements for fourteen cost centres throughout the organisation.

The system that we use has been adapted to meet our special needs. Our products are manufactured under a wide variety of processes, some under flow production, some under batch production, some in twos and threes.

In addition we have a substantial resale section. The special features of the system that we have devised are described in Appendix 3.1. They may be interesting to others who have similarly diverse businesses.

The statement of account serves the same indispensable function as the sextant serves to the mariner. It tells us where we are. But it does not tell us where we are going, how things are changing. This vital information is best shown by graphs. In Fig. 3.1 the sales, the profit and the net worth (or share-

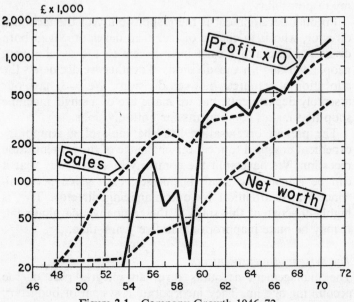

Figure **3.1** Company Growth 1946–72

holders' equity) of the company are shown over the whole life of the company on semi-logarithmic graph paper. When the results are plotted in this way a straight line represents a constant percentage rate of growth. A graph may give very misleading results unless it extends over a long enough period. In Fig. 3.2 the sales of our first group of products are shown after the values have been reduced to 1960 prices. Comparison with UK steel production shows the cause of the cyclic variation of sales and the slow rate of growth of the volume of the sales of this group of products.

But Fig. 3.1 is the key to the financial history of the company. It shows how in the first decade the sales in-

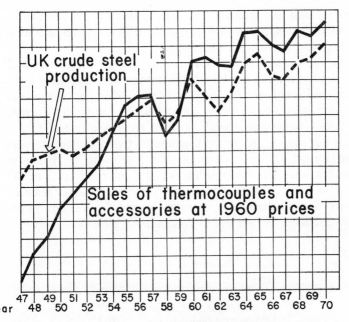

Figure 3.2   Fluctuations in Sales of Thermocouples and Accessories
and UK Steel Production 1947–70

creased rapidly, but the profits were not adequate to build up
the net worth fast enough to match the growth of the sales.
Consequently we ran into overtrading and had to turn to
ICFC for financial help.

Between 1960 and 1966 the sales increased only slowly but
the profits were excellent. The net worth increased much
faster than the sales and we accumulated sufficient cash to
pay off our ICFC loan and build a new, larger factory
without further financial help.

Between 1966 and 1971 sales grew rapidly once again, but
this time the net worth grew at about the same rate and both
more than doubled. We had neither a cash problem nor any
serious danger of a surtax direction because the rate of
growth of sales and the return on capital were compatible.

Our experience has impressed upon us the importance of
compatibility between growth and profitability. We have

looked into this question and have written down the conditions of compatibility that exist under different circumstances. The report is included as Appendix 3.2.

We set ourselves targets of profitability and of growth and we make sure that the targets are compatible. Our targets are that we should make a profit before tax of 20 per cent on the total assets of the company (before deducting current liabilities) and that the sales should grow at a rate of 15 per cent per annum. It can best be shown that these two targets are compatible for our company by expressing the figures in the balance sheet and trading account as percentages of the annual sales value. In this form the balance sheet remains pretty well unchanged from year to year. Typical figures for our company are set out as follows:

P & L Account

Sales	100%
Trading profit	14·0%
Less interest on loan	0·2%
Profit before tax	13·8%
Less corporation tax	5·8%
Profit after tax	8·0%
Distributed to shareholders	1·6%
Retained in business	6·4%

Balance sheet (expressed as percentages of annual sales)

Liabilities		Assets	
Shareholders equity	44%	Fixed assets	30%
Tax due	6%	Stock and work in progress	18%a
Creditors and provisions	14%	Debtors	22%
Bank overdraft	6%		
Total liabilities	70%	Total assets	70%

a work in progress at prime cost

It will be seen that the trading profit is 20 per cent of the total assets and the profit retained in the business, after distributing one-fifth of the net profits to the shareholders, is sufficient to increase the shareholders' equity by 15 per cent. This increase is, of course, sufficient to support an increase in sales of 15 per cent provided that the fixed assets, stock, debtors, creditors etc. also increase in the same proportion, which in general they will do. It is an interesting feature of this method of presenting the accounts that several important business ratios appear at once and others are easily deduced. Fig. 3.3 shows the way that several important business ratios have changed during the life of the company.

It will be noticed that it became much more difficult to retain a good ratio of profits to total assets when we moved to the new factory, not because of lack of profits, but because the expensive new factory increased the value of the fixed assets. We are coming to think that it is best to set the target of profit as a percentage of the net assets in which fixed assets are written up to present-day values. The appendices are based on the use of this criterion.

The ratio that has remained the most constant is the ratio of profit to added value. For this purpose I have defined added value simply as profit plus wages and salaries. During the first ten years of the history of the company, resale formed a larger proportion of total sales than it has done in later years. We naturally made a smaller percentage profit on our sales in those days, but in the profitable years 1955 and 1956 the ratio of profit to added value reached the sort of values that we have made during the sixties. Broadly, we have maintained a ratio of 1 : 2 between profits and wages and salaries. The ratio of product development expenditure to profit has risen during the sixties. We now reckon that we should spend an amount equal to about half the profit before tax. We think that an expenditure of this order of magnitude is necessary to produce sufficient growth to match the rate of accumulation of capital—i.e. about 15 per cent per annum.

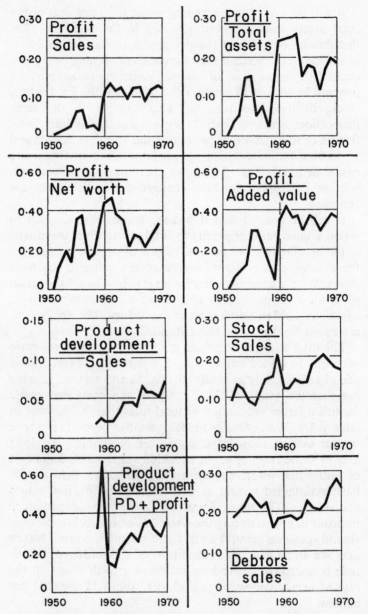

Figure 3.3   Changes in Eight Business Ratios 1950–70

Operating the system
We learnt in 1959, when we had to take ruthless decisions and to dispense with the services of one director, that it is not helpful to disguise the fact that power lies where the shares are held. All directors are equal, but Eric and I are more equal than the others because we control between us more than 50 per cent of the equity. Fortunately we are sufficiently different in outlook and abilities to be able to make one good man of all-round ability.

We think that there is much to be said for having a bit of extra capacity at the top. We are usually both pretty busy; but if an important matter of policy needs a decision we have time to discuss it together in detail and at leisure. Since we usually start from rather different viewpoints we have a decent chance of reaching a sound decision by this method.

We have a quarterly board meeting at which we discuss the financial results for the quarter and matters arising from the financial figures. The board is, in our case, indistinguishable from the executive committee, and meets to discuss all matters of general policy as and when the need arises.

The two divisions are run on a rather personal small-company basis. Each has a regular meeting every month of sales engineers, product development people and production manager to discuss opportunities and problems of mutual interest. This is the primary vehicle of communication within a division. Salesmen of the metals industries division attend the meeting of the radiation division to keep themselves informed and to pass on news.

THE DEVELOPMENT PLAN

Product development has two objectives. First, it should ensure that the company rarely, if ever, needs to seek business by cutting profit margins below acceptable levels. We should be able to let such business go if it is not profitable, knowing that we have new and profitable products coming into production to replace what we lose. Secondly, product development should ensure that the sales of the company expand at a rate compatible with the accumulation of capital.

E

It is not too difficult to develop new products. The principal problem is the choice of suitable products to develop. The new product should have potential sales that are big enough to make a significant addition to the sales: but the potential sales should also not be too big. The cost of developing and launching a new product is generally related to the potential sales. If we tackle a product whose sales are too large we are likely to find ourselves competing with firms having much greater development capacity than our own, who can afford to spend more on the development. Such a competitor has the resources to produce a better product, to produce it faster and to promote it with a bigger sales force. And if we got the business we might not be able to finance it.

Secondly, the product must be well designed and acceptable to the customer. This implies that we should ideally develop products for the markets that we understand thoroughly, using technology in which we have first-class expertise. We should never attempt developments in which we do not have either the knowledge of the market or the technical expertise in a high degree. If we have only one, we must acquire the other either through careful market research or by engaging people with the right knowledge.

Finally, the product should be one which shows promise of a better-than-average profit on sales. This is possible if there is a good patent protection or if we are technically well ahead of our competitors. Ideally one should be the only supplier of any consequence. I sometimes explain that if I had a little goat I would tether it in a secluded corner of the field where the grass grows lush and green and where the bigger animals do not trouble to come.

Finding new products

How do good products get developed? We have looked carefully at this history of our better lines and the interesting fact is that most of them came to us. The British Coal Utilisation Research Association wanted to measure the temperature of the hot gases in the boilers of power stations. The head of the department concerned knew us and asked us to develop a suction pyrometer. Pilkington Brothers asked us to develop a radiation pyrometer to measure the temperature of hot glass. They came to us because we had shown them our new surface pyrometer. In these cases a customer brought us his problem and we had to possess the technical expertise to find solutions to them and devise products to meet the customers' needs.

In other cases a fully developed product is brought to us. The outstanding example of this is the disposable liquid steel thermocouple. The European manager of the American company brought it to us and asked us if we would like to make it under licence. He had visited British steel companies who had recommended us to him.

Other products are brought to us in the prototype stage. A research association brought us an instrument to measure the dew point (i.e. the moisture content) of hot gases. We retained the measuring element unchanged, but redesigned the probe in which it was mounted. We made a more professional-looking case for the meters and put in an amplifier so that more rugged meters could be used. We have an arrangement with the International Flame Research Foundation whereby we put the instruments that they develop through a similar process and make them available to their members.

In a minority of instances we think up a new product, believing that it will find a market. When silicon solar cells were invented they were used to convert sunlight into electricity. The big flaps that open out from a space vehicle when it goes into orbit are covered with solar cells that recharge the vehicle's batteries from the sunlight. When I saw the technical characteristics of the cell I guessed that it was exactly suitable as a detector in a radiation pyrometer. We proceeded to build a new series of radiation pyrometers based on the silicon cell, which now forms the greater part of our sales in this area. But we have noticed that we are rather less successful with products that we develop on this basis. There seems to be a larger chance of producing a product for which there is not much of a market. This may be because a product of this kind may be sold in markets that we do not know sufficiently well. We sometimes think that we spend all this money on research and development, but the real winners often come to us from outside. This is no reason for cutting back our efforts. The products come to us because we are known to have technical expertise of a high order in certain areas.

It is important to analyse the situation and to find out why good products do come to us. What are the flowers that attract the butterflies to us and bring new life and growth with them? It could be said to be the company image. It is our reputation for good service and rugged, dependable products. But to this must be added the lectures that we give to technical societies, the articles in the technical press, exhibits at conferences and exhibitions and the quality of the technical men who visit our customers and discuss their problems with them. We have to be good, but we also have to be seen to be good; there must be flowers to attract the butterflies.

There is no need to be despondent if one is not first in the market with a product. The disposable liquid steel thermocouple was developed in America because American high labour costs favoured a product of relatively high first cost but low maintenance cost. The American company that introduced it here did all the hard work in convincing the British user that the method was also better than the old method under British conditions. We came in several years later. But, with first-class service, a good product and a good reputation, we quickly took as much of the market as we think we should have.

Selecting products for development

Product development is an open-ended activity. There is no limit to the amount that can justifiably be spent on promising new products. But there is a limit to the funds available. It is most important to spend the limited funds in the most productive way possible. This involves concentration. There is a great temptation to spread the available resources too thinly and this must be resisted.

Concentration of resources is one of the great principles

of business. The sales effort must be concentrated on the customers and on the products that can give large orders, substantial sales and good profit margins. Improvements in manufacturing technique must be concentrated on products with substantial volume of production in which big improvements are possible. Similarly the effort in product development must be concentrated on the right products. We have found that hunch and flair are not sufficiently good guides to deciding on the right products to develop, although they play a big part. Our biggest mistakes have been in misjudging the market or in spending much more on development than the sales would justify. We are beginning to make use of market research. This is new to us and we are feeling our way. Industrial market research is notoriously difficult, not least because the customer does not know what he wants. It is only when you give him something and ask him to buy it that you can get very definite information. But undoubtedly market research has a part to play, particularly in markets that we do not know too well.

How much to spend
We have tried to decide how we should spend on any particular development. The results of our thinking are set out in Appendix 3.3. This analysis gives us a rule-of-thumb answer. We can usually justify expenditure up to one-fifth of the annual sales that the product will in due course attain. We notice that many new products soon begin to produce sales, but the volume only builds up slowly and it will typically take four or five years before the sales level off at a relatively constant value. The life of a product is very variable, but it is typically ten to twenty years—say fifteen years. This is a very crude model of the sales development which is different in every case. But the whole exercise is very crude indeed and the model is adequate.

We have to take account of the fact that we may not succeed in making an acceptable product at the right price and that if product and price are right the customer may decide that he wants something different after all. So after guessing the size of the potential market we multiply it by a factor which is our estimate of the probability of success. If we reckon we have a 50 : 50 chance we halve the potential market and so on. Then we have to take account of competition.

If, for example, we believe that there is a market for 200,000 of a product per annum at a price of 50p each then the potential market is £100,000 per annum. If we reckon that we have a 40 per cent chance of success this reduces the market to £40,000, of which we would expect to get say 50 per cent, making £20,000 per annum. Such a product would justify an expenditure of one-fifth of this annual sales total, i.e. £4,000.

This analysis assumes that we can expect to sell the product at such a price as to be able to make a profit of 20 per cent on our capital plus 5 per cent on the selling price to contribute to development costs. If the price is not critical we may be able to contribute more than 5 per cent, in which case we could justify an expenditure of perhaps £10,000.

Using this criterion we have begun to make a regular assessment of our development projects. The assessment of the potential market changes greatly from month to month and we may for this reason close down one project and transfer extra effort to another. We hope to be able to make forward planning estimates of sales in the next few years from products that we are developing. This will be integrated into an overall development plan.

We have been thinking about this development plan for some years. We are at last beginning to see how it should be done and we aim to make a start on it in the near future.

HUMAN RELATIONS

To show our appreciation of the excellent cooperation we had in the reorganisation of the company in the crisis years of 1957–8 we shared part of the increased profits with all our employees, giving them a Christmas bonus which has been a regular feature ever since. We pay out something between 10 and 15 per cent of the annual wage or salary according to the profitability of the year's work. The bonus is in fact calculated and announced each quarter and is now paid quarterly to some, annually to others.

At about this time we also introduced a cost-of-living increment. It seemed obvious to us that it was dishonest to pretend that we were giving a 7 per cent increase in wages or salary when 5 per cent of it might reflect only a change in the value of money. So at the beginning of October all wages and salaries are now adjusted automatically to take account of the change in the retail price index since the previous year. This makes our thinking about remuneration much simpler and more realistic. We count it as common honesty.

Some time later we began to introduce the principle of 'no second-class citizens'. As far as possible the man on the shopfloor is treated in the same way as the office staff, paid a standard weekly wage, has his pay made up if he is sick, has holidays calculated on the same formula, is free to join the staff pension scheme and so on. It is not always easy to get a minority of our new recruits to accept the responsibilities that these privileges entail, but the effort is well worth while.

BUSINESS TRUTHS

There are a few principles that we have read or have found out for ourselves that we think are worth setting down or repeating. Here are a few:

1. Perhaps the most important is Parkinson's Law; and the man who laughs loudest may be the man to whom it most applies. So here it is once more: work expands to fill the available time; expenditure grows to absorb the available income.
2. A company will grow if it builds on its strengths. And remember that these strengths change, sometimes quite quickly.
3. Every executive should know what are the few things that he does well.
4. Concentrate effort where it will produce big results.
5. There are only two kinds of people—those that pro-

duce results and those that produce excellent reasons why the results are not forthcoming.

6. Risks must be taken in business; but no risk should be big enough to cripple the business if it failed.
7. Don't think that you know all the answers. There are excellent people around to help and advise you.
8. Look at the company through the customer's eyes.
9. An entrepreneur is a man who knows an opportunity when he sees one—and takes it.
10. The man who is second in the market often gets the lion's share at half the cost.
11. The real wealth of a company is knowledge. Knowledge must therefore be actively enlarged by all means.

A System of Management Accounts designed for a Mixed-Product Company

A few years ago we realised that as the business grew it would no longer be possible for the directors to keep a close watch on the day-to-day operations of the various departments. It was decided to delegate the responsibility for running the various sections of the business to second-line managers. Each department became a cost centre and each manager receives a quarterly financial statement for his department.

At the same time we were also aware that we needed a more systematic appraisal of the contributions that the different product groups were making to the profits of the company. Our products range from resale items through job production and batch production to items produced on a basis of flow production at a rate of a million pieces a year. Some products need a large sales effort, other very little. It would be all too easy for the profits from some products to drain away through undetected losses on others.

To meet these two needs, we devised a system of control accounts to suit our particular business. The starting point of this system is the company's profit and growth objectives.

Our objectives are that the company should make 20 per cent profit on its net assets before tax and that, after paying out one-fifth of its profits to the shareholders, the profits should be applied to financing a growth of 15 per cent per annum in the sales of the company. Inflation has been running until recently at about 3 per cent per annum, so the objective implies a real growth rate of about 12 per cent per annum. It will be seen from Appendix 3.1 that these two objectives are compatible at a reasonable borrowing ratio, provided that the assets are valued at present-day prices.

It was decided that the requirement to make 20 per cent on the .capital should be applied at the points at which capital was invested. It is just as important to avoid excessive investment in stocks, wasted space, unused machinery or uncollected debts as it is to make a good profit margin on the sales. The cost centres are therefore charged 20 per cent per annum for the use of money.

The same principle is applied to the costing system. Since we consider the use of money to involve cost, the 20 per cent charge for its use is included among the overheads that are applied to direct labour on an hourly rate. Consequently we derive, not the factory cost of a product, but the 'factory price', which includes an increment of profit appropriate to the capital employed in production.

The whole system is incorporated in an annual budget in which we forecast the probable performance of the company during the coming financial year. Before the year begins we make sure that the targets that we are setting ourselves will result in an adequate profit and an adequate cash flow to meet the capital expenditure proposed. During the year we can then concentrate our attention on deviations from the budget. We prepare quarterly accounts for the board and quarterly responsibility accounting statements for the second-line managers. We also prepare an annual profit statement that shows the profit made on each product group above (or below) 20 per cent on net assets. There is also an annual contribution statement showing the contribution made by each product before the deduction of fixed costs.

THE QUARTERLY ACCOUNTS

Each quarter we prepare a trading account and a balance sheet. We also have a company sales analysis, and a company profit analysis. In the profit analysis the sales and gross profit margins are set out for the different product groups and are compared with the budget figures. The selling expenses, product development costs and other overhead expenses are also presented in the same way.

In every case a charge of 20 per cent for the use of money is included among the expenses incurred in manufacturing or in other activities. The profit analysis therefore leads to a statement showing the excess (or deficit) of the company profit above (or below) 20 per cent on the assets.

The chief accountant in drawing up the profit analysis writes comments beside each category of product or expense, such as 'financial future not good, management action needed' or 'continuing high activity producing profits beyond budget expectations'.

These accounts are carefully studied by the board and form

the basis of any action that may be needed to correct the course of the company.

The budget is not, of course, imposed from above. It comes up from the second-line managers. When the system was introduced we realised how important it was to ensure that they were aware that the system was not imposed by top management. We were careful to explain to them what we were trying to achieve and full and frank discussions were held with each of the managers who are responsible for the fourteen cost centres.

Each year our budgets for the following year are prepared. Commencing with the sales budget, which is the responsibility of the sales manager, each manager assesses what his department will require in terms of capital, labour and expenses to meet the budgeted sales. It is during this budget exercise that managers are encouraged to plan for an improvement in the performance of their department, and to set themselves certain goals for the following year. Each manager discusses his proposals individually with his superior before submitting them to the chief accountant for incorporating in the budget.

The responsibility accounting statement is given to the managers quarterly. The statement lists the direct labour, materials, and the cost centre overheads, which the manager is expected to control. It also lists, for information, the allocated expenses, which he cannot control; and the money used in buildings, plant, furniture, vehicles, stock and work in progress. Each of the above items is compared with the budget figure, which was agreed with the manager during the budget exercise.

A statement presented in this form enables the departmental manager to control closely the expenses of his department. Costs are best controlled by the man closest to their incidence. He can see from the statement which costs are large enough to warrant extra effort being expended to give a better control. In some departments labour is the expensive item and in others it is material. In the former case the manager knows that he must concentrate on good production methods first, and in the latter keen buying is essential.

We feel that the introduction of responsibility accounts, coupled with budgetary control, has produced the following advantages:

1. It has made us define clear areas of responsibility.
2. We have been encouraged to plan the year's work as a team.
3. Managers have been made aware of costs, both visible and hidden.
4. It has made it possible to control costs 'on the spot' and to watch them effectively.
5. Managers have a greater interest in their work because more responsibility has been given to them.
6. It has made it easier to spot a manager's weaknesses, and give training where necessary.
7. We believe that it has increased respect for the senior management for delegating responsibility, and at the same time demanding effective financial performance within that area of delegated responsibility.

THE ANNUAL PROFIT STATEMENT

The object of the profit statement is to show, as nearly as possible, how much profit is being made on each group of products. There are limits to the degree to which the products can be separated. For example, the fact that product X is being sold may enable product Y to be sold in the same market at very little extra cost. Nevertheless a real and meaningful division of costs is possible at an adequate level of precision.

An example of the profit statement is shown at the end of this appendix. Although the figures are fictitious they are typical of the varied costs and margins that occur in our business. The first two product groups are resale items and the other two are manufactured products. We take care to divide the products into relatively homogeneous groups. This occurs without any trouble for manufactured products; the products that we buy and resell have to be grouped with some care.

It has already been explained that we aim to determine the 'factory price' of a product, not its factory cost. Since the factory price includes a charge for the use of money it is exactly comparable with the cost of the products that we buy for resale. Indeed, if an employee wished to take home a pyrometer to give to his wife for her birthday he could have it at the 'factory price' provided that he paid cash and packed it up himself in his own time.

We can therefore record both manufactured and resale items in the same column headed 'Gross margin after 20 per cent on manufacturing assets', knowing that they represent exactly comparable margins. We then proceed to split the company on-costs between the product groups.

Once again we incorporate in, say, selling costs a charge for the use of the money invested in company cars, office space etc. used in the sales department.

The home sales expenses are added in separately at the end so that we can see the costs of exported goods. Both types of sales require the same sort of order handling procedure, which includes processing the customer's order, making out works orders, preparing the invoice, packing and despatching the goods. We consider that the cost of operation does not depend very much on the value of the invoice and we allocate the order handling costs on a basis of so much per invoice.

We then add in a charge for the use of money invested in finished stocks, and a charge for the use of money required to finance the difference between the debtors and creditors. This latter charge is allocated in proportion to the value of the sales in each product group. This total gives us a figure for the overhead expenses and use of money involved in an export sale.

The home sales costs are allocated by the sales manager to the product groups on a basis of records kept by the sales engineers of the products discussed with each customer. There is a wide variation between products. In this analysis it is important to split the sales into product groups of roughly equal size, otherwise there is certain to be an excessive allocation of sales costs to the small product groups.

It may be noticed that we do not have a column for administration expenses, i.e. the managing directors, the chief accountant and the few people that work directly for them. We consider that in the final analysis the function of these people is to maximise the return on the company's money. These administration expenses are therefore allocated to the various cost centres throughout the company in proportion to the amount of money that they use.

The analysis allows us to determine the mark-up on each product group that just brings in 20 per cent on the capital employed. This enables us to fix minimum selling prices to customers at home and abroad. Subsidiary companies are charged factory price plus 10 per cent, to cover order handling and the use of money tied up during transport of the goods to the overseas company. It must be emphasised that these prices are minimum selling prices. The actual selling price is determined by market conditions. It is essential that we should get more than the minimum price wherever we can do so, because nothing has yet been provided for product development. The last column shows the variance above the minimum 20 per cent profit on assets employed. It will be seen that some products produce a much better margin than others, but none is substantially below zero.

We do not consider that product development costs can be allocated to any particular product groups. The profits on today's winners must be devoted to the development of tomorrow's winners, which may be products of a very different kind. So we catch what we can where we can and spend it as wisely as we know how; and its wise spending is very difficult indeed.

We have produced the profit statement quarterly, but now we realise that we have all that we need for current control purposes in the simpler profit analysis. In future the profit statement will be prepared annually. During the two years that we have had it we have used it for several important purposes. Some of them are listed below.

1. We watch the profitability of each product group and review the pricing policy if any group falls below the norm.
2. It is an excellent basis for fixing prices of new products. We can readily find the factory price and then estimate the order handling costs (what will the average invoice value be?), the cost of finished stock holding, if any, and the selling costs (which existing product group will it resemble?) and finally add 3 per cent for debtors-less-creditors. This gives us a good minimum price. We know that we can usually get 10 per cent more and a good product will usually stand at least 25 per cent more than the minimum price. Without these extra margins we could do no product development and the future of the company would be bleak.
3. We can decide whether it is profitable to buy a component from an outside supplier or continue to make it ourselves. However, we might need to look at marginal costs in some cases.
4. If we want to fix a price to a reseller who buys in quantities we can see what we save in selling costs and in the fact that we need not carry stocks. This helps most if we are in a position in which we need to get down to a low price, perhaps for a large overseas agent.
5. When we sell to a subsidiary company we know that we can sell at factory price plus 10 per cent. At this price we take

the correct margin in the parent company to make a proper return on the capital employed here. The subsidiary can then fix a proper selling price for the overseas market.

6. We know how much to add to our prices to a customer who takes extended credit or how much we can allow to a customer (and it does happen) who pays in advance.

7. We can quickly tell whether it is worthwhile to buy cheaply in bulk, and how much to add on to the price of slow-moving stocks.

ANNUAL PROFIT STATEMENT

Company on-costs including use of money

Product group:	Sales £×1,000	Sales %	Gross margin after 20% on manufacturing assets £×1,000	Gross margin %	Order handling £×1,000	Order handling %	Finished stock £×1,000	Finished stock %	Debtors less creditors £×1,000	Debtors less creditors %	Expenses total %	Home Sales costs £×1,000	Home Sales costs %	Home total costs %	Minimum mark-up for home sales %	Actual mark-up %	Profit variance above 20% on assets £×1,000	Profit variance above 20% on assets %
A	93·7	100	30·3	33	5·0	5	7·8	8	2·8	3	17	6·9	7	24	36	48	+7·9	+8
B	89·9	100	11·3	12½	2·6	3	3·7	4	2·6	3	10	2·2	2½	12½	14	14	+0·2	+0
C	141·7	100	52·4	37	4·4	3	0·3	0	4·2	3	6	11·7	14	20	32	59	+31·9	+23
D	152·4	100	15·8	10	6·7	4½	0·7	½	4·5	3	8	5·8	5	13	14	12	−1·9	−1

E+c.

Compatible Targets of Growth and Profit for the Small Company

A small business must provide sufficient finance from its profits to sustain its growth. It will not necessarily need to provide the whole of the extra capital because some can be raised by borrowing, either from the bank or from financial institutions such as ICFC. But if it does not provide at least half the extra capital it will be difficult to raise the remainder by borrowing. Of course, temporarily rapid growth can be accommodated for a few years by increasing the proportion that is borrowed. But over an extended period the company must either generate a proper proportion of its own financial requirements or issue additional shares.

Issuing extra shares is a simple matter for a large public company with a good profit record. For a small company it may be impossible or it may involve the risk that control of the company may slip out of the hands of the owners. This is reasonably and properly considered to be unacceptable by many small companies.

It is therefore a very important question to ask how fast a company can safely grow and how the rate of growth is related to the profitability. It is easy to derive a simple mathematical formula that answers all aspects of this important question.

The net assets of a company are financed partly by the shareholders' equity (issued shares and reserves) and partly by money borrowed from the bank or from other financial institutions. We will call the ratio of the borrowed money to the shareholders' equity the 'borrowing ratio' and give it the symbol b. If the net assets of the company financed by these two means are A, then we can write:

$$\text{Shareholder's equity} = \frac{A}{1+b}$$

$$\text{Money borrowed} = \frac{bA}{1+b}$$

$$\therefore \text{ Net assets} = \frac{A}{1+b} + \frac{bA}{1+b} = A$$

F

Let us assume that the company always makes an annual profit at a rate p (or $100p\%$) on the net assets. So the profit before tax is pA. When the company gets bigger and its assets reach a value $2A$ we assume that the profits grow in proportion and become $2pA$, and so on.

But the company has borrowed an amount $\dfrac{bA}{1+b}$ on which it has to pay interest at a rate r (or $100r\%$). We must deduct this interest from the profit, so that we are left with a net profit before tax of:

$$pA - \frac{rbA}{1+b}$$

If the profit is taxed at a rate t (or $100t\%$), the profit after tax is:

$$A(1-t)\left\{ p - \frac{rb}{1+b} \right\}$$

Now the company is growing and for the sake of simplicity we assume that every year it increases by a fraction g. This means that we need extra capital to finance the assets that have grown from $A/(1+g)$ to A. In fact we need an extra amount $Ag/(1+g)$. If we are going to maintain the same borrowing ratio the part of this extra capital that must be provided by the shareholders' equity is:

$$\frac{Ag}{(1+b)(1+g)}$$

The condition that this amount is exactly provided by the profits retained in the business is expressed by writing:

$$\frac{Ag}{(1+b)(1+g)} = A(1-f)(1-t)\left\{ p - \frac{rb}{1+b} \right\}$$

$$\therefore \quad \frac{g}{1+g} = (1-f)(1-t)(p+pb-rb)$$

This simple equation answers all the questions that can be raised about profitability, growth and borrowing ratio.

It must be emphasised that the equation gives the equilibrium condition of the system. This is to say that the borrowing ratio, for example, will in due course attain the value calculated from the equation if the rate of growth always has a particular value and the profitability is always the same and the same fraction of the profits is always paid out to the shareholders.

Of course this never happens in a real business. Everything changes all the time. Growth accelerates or slows down, profitability improves and declines and so on. But this does not invalidate the calculations. It merely means that the business moves every year towards a new equilibrium condition. We can say at any time 'If things go on like this we shall some day need no overdraft', or 'If things continue like this we shall need a borrowing ratio of 2—we are heading for trouble'.

Above all, the calculations allow managers of small businesses to set compatible targets of profit and growth. It is no good having a target of doubling the business every five years unless we can see at the same time exactly how the growth can be financed. These calculations give us the targets of profit that are compatible with any particular target of growth.

Tables 3.1 to 3.4 show the values of the rates of annual growth that can be financed by different rates of profit on the net assets, as they have been defined above. The growth rates are given as percentages per annum for different borrowing ratios. The first table shows what is possible if all the profits are left in the business; the other tables show what can be done if various fractions of the net profit after tax are paid out to the shareholders.

RATES OF GROWTH COMPATIBLE WITH VARIOUS
PROFITABILITIES

Table 3.1   All profits retained in the business

Borrowing ratio:	Profit on net assets				
	15%	20%	25%	30%	35%
0·0	9	13	17	21	25
0·2	10	15	20	25	30
0·4	11	17	22	29	36
0·6	12	18	25	33	42
0·8	13	20	28	38	48
1·0	14	22	32	43	56

Table 3.2   One-fifth of profits paid to shareholders

Borrowing ratio:	Profit on net assets				
	15%	20%	25%	30%	35%
0·0	7	10	13	16	19
0·2	8	11	15	19	23
0·4	9	13	17	22	27
0·6	10	14	19	25	31
0·8	10	16	22	28	35
1·0	11	17	24	31	40

Table 3.3   One-third of profits paid to shareholders

	Profit on net assets				
Borrowing ratio:	15%	20%	25%	30%	35%
0·0	6	8	10	13	16
0·2	7	9	12	15	19
0·4	7	11	14	18	22
0·6	8	12	16	20	25
0·8	9	13	17	22	28
1·0	9	14	19	25	31

Table 3.4   One-half of profits paid to shareholders

	Profit on net assets				
Borrowing ratio:	15%	20%	25%	30%	35%
0·0	4	6	8	9	11
0·2	5	7	9	11	13
0·4	5	8	10	12	15
0·6	6	9	11	14	17
0·8	6	9	12	16	19
1·0	7	10	14	18	22

The calculations have been based on the assumption that interest must be paid on the money that has been borrowed at a rate of 8 per cent per annum, and that corporation tax is levied at a rate of 42½ per cent. These exact values are not critical in the calculations.

THE EFFECT OF INFLATION

In times of inflation it is important, before using the tables, to subtract from the profit shown in the financial accounts any fictitious profit that is derived from the increase in the money value of the assets due to inflation during the financial year. It is this real profit that should be used. Furthermore it is important to ensure that the value of the 'net assets' that is used is the value at present prices, not the historic cost.

But this is not the whole story. In times of inflation it may be necessary to make additional profit over and above the values shown in the tables if the borrowing ratio is to remain constant. This additional profit is needed to provide the extra working capital that is needed to operate the company that starts and finishes the financial year with identically the same fixed assets and the same physical stock and work in progress. But at the end of the year, as a result of inflation, all the assets are valued in the books at a higher value than they were at the beginning of the year, all being increased by a factor $(1 + i)$. In this case we would say that the rate of inflation is $100i$ per cent per annum.

At the end of the year the value of the buildings has increased from say B to $(1 + i)B$: the increment iB may be added to the general reserve so increasing the book value of the shareholder's equity. This fictitious profit is not subject to corporation tax.

The other fixed assets (F) and the stock and work in progress (S) are shown at the year-end at a value $(1 + i)(F + S)$. This fictitious profit $i(F + S)$ is subject to corporation tax at a rate of $100t\%$. (In fact some of the increase in the fixed assets will come from increased depreciation, but the effect on our calculations is marginal.) Consequently we may only add the untaxed residue $i(1 - t)$ $(F + S)$ to the shareholders' equity. The remainder, $it(F + S)$, must be provided either from profits or by borrowing.

Similarly the debtors D will rise to $(1 + i)D$. But on the other side of the balance sheet the creditors C will rise to $(1 + i)C$. The difference $(D - C)$ increases by $i(D - C)$ and this increment must also be financed either out of profits or by borrowing. It should be noticed that this increment must be financed from *taxed* profits, so that the untaxed profits required would be $i(D - C)/(1 - t)$.

If we exclude financing by borrowed money (i.e. the borrowing ratio is zero) then it is necessary to provide extra profits equal, before tax, to:

$$i \left\{ t(F + S) + \frac{D - C}{1 - t} \right\}$$

If inflation is running at 10 per cent per annum, this extra profit would typically be about 5 per cent of the net assets.

But we have said that the extra finance can be provided by borrowing. The fictitious profits on the fixed assets, stock and work in progress increase the book value of the shareholders' equity by:

$$i \left\{ B + (1 - t)(F + S) \right\}$$

The net assets have increased from A to $(1 + i)A$. If the borrowing ratio remains unchanged at b then the increase in the shareholders' equity must also be equal to:

$$\frac{iA}{1 + b}$$

If these two expressions are equal it will be found that the borrowing ratio b is given by

$$b = \frac{A}{B + (1 - t)(F + S)} - 1$$

This is the smallest value of the borrowing ratio for which all the extra capital needed to finance the inflationary increase in assets can be provided by borrowing, without increasing the borrowing ratio and without using any of the profits. If the borrowing ratio were higher, then a higher rate of true (non-inflationary) growth would be possible under inflationary conditions than under conditions of steady money values. But this is rather an academic point because the borrowing ratios required would usually be in excess of $0 \cdot 65$, which is rather too high for comfort.

It is interesting to notice that this critical borrowing ratio is independent of the rate of inflation.

If anyone is surprised that a company can be better off under inflationary conditions, he should think of the man with a 90 per cent mortgage on his house. If house prices rise he can make a substantial profit if he sells his house again and pockets the proceeds after paying off the mortgage. Unfortunately, he usually needs another—and larger—house!

A Theory of Product Development Expenditure

We need some rule-of-thumb method to decide whether a new product should be developed and whether the work on a particular project should be continued or terminated. The basis of the criterion must be whether the sales that will be generated will be sufficient to justify the expenditure.

We may analyse the problem for two different accounting methods. Either the research expenditure may be capitalised and recovered from future sales using discounted cash flow; or the expenditure may be written off in the year in which it is incurred. In the first method we must choose a rate of interest for the DCF calculation. Since we aim to make 20 per cent profit on our assets we will assume a rate of interest of 20 per cent. We will assume that the product has a life of fifteen years. In the second method we shall find it necessary to assume a rate of growth, which we will take to be 15 per cent per annum.

1. CAPITALISE THE PD EXPENSE

After n years an investment of £1 at $100p\%$ compound interest is worth $£(1 + p)^n$. Consequently an income of £1 received n years hence is only worth $£(1 + p)^n$ today. An annual income of £1 per annum for fifteen years is therefore worth today $£T$, where:

$$T = 1 + \frac{1}{1+p} + \frac{1}{(1+p)}^2 + \ldots + \frac{1}{(1+p)}^{14}$$

This is a geometric progression and we may find the value of T in the usual way by dividing T by $(1 + p)$ giving:

$$\frac{T}{1+p} = \frac{1}{1+p} + \frac{1}{(1+p)}^2 + \ldots + \frac{1}{(1+p)}^{14} + \frac{1}{(1+p)}^{15}$$

Subtracting the second equation from the first gives:

$$T\left\{1 - \frac{1}{1+p}\right\} = 1 - \frac{1}{(1+p)}^{15}$$

or

$$T = \left\{1 + \frac{1}{p}\right\}\left\{1 - \frac{1}{(1+p)}^{15}\right\}$$

Taking $p = 0\cdot20$ we find that:

$$T = 6\{1 - 1/(1\cdot2)^{15}\}$$
$$= 5\cdot60$$

If the sales had continued indefinitely the value of T would have been $6\cdot0$ instead of $5\cdot6$, so the exact life of the product is not important.

If we assume that we can set aside a fraction f of the annual sales value S to pay for product development, the total value today of the return from the fifteen years' sales is $5\cdot60fS$. If it had been necessary to wait for, say, four years before beginning to sell the product, then the value of the return from sales would have been reduced by a factor of $1\cdot4^4$, i.e. to $2\cdot70fS$.

If we assume that $f = 0\cdot05$ (i.e. we can afford to set aside 5 per cent of the sales value to pay for the cost of development) then the total return is equivalent to $0\cdot28S$, or if we have to wait four years for the sales to begin, the total return is equivalent to $0\cdot14S$.

We conclude therefore that if we require a return of 20 per cent on our capital, the cost of development should not exceed $0\cdot28$ times the annual sales if the sales commence at once, or $0\cdot14$ times the annual sales if the sales do not begin until four years later.

2. EXPENDITURE WRITTEN OFF IN THE YEAR INCURRED

If we use this basis of accounting then we do not need to consider discounted cash flow. But we do need to know the rate of growth of the sales. Let us assume that the expenditure on product development increases at a rate of $100g\%$ per annum. Let us suppose that the investment made in any one year produces no sales in the first four years but that in the fifth year it begins to generate a constant annual volume of sales equal to N times the investment and that this volume continues unchanged for fifteen years and then abruptly ceases. Let the investment in year zero be D_0, then we have:

Year	PD expenditure (D)	Resulting sales (S)
0	D_0	0
1	$(1+g)D_0$	0
2	$(1+g)^2 D_0$	0
3	$(1+g)^3 D_0$	0
4	$(1+g)^4 D_0$	ND_0
5	$(1+g)^5 D_0$	$ND_0\{1+(1+g)\}$
6	$(1+g)_0 D_0$	$ND_0\{1+(1+g)+(1+g)^2\}$

. . . .

| 18 | $(1+g)^{18} D_0$ | $ND_0\{1+(1+g)+(1+g)^2+\ldots+(1+g)^{14}\}$ |

$$= \frac{ND_0\{(1+g)^{15}-1\}}{g}$$

| 19 | $(1+g)^{19} D_0$ | $ND_0\{(1+g)+(1+g)^2+\ldots+(1+g)^{15}\}$ |

$$= \frac{ND_0(1+g)\{(1+g)^{15}-1\}}{g}$$

. . . .

The value of sales at the eighteenth and nineteenth years are again the sum of a geometric series and are calculated by the simple formula derived in the previous section. It will be seen that after the eighteenth year the ratio of the expenditure on product development (D) to the sales (S) in the same year attains a constant value given by

$$\frac{D}{S} = \frac{g(1+g)^{18}}{N\{(1+g)^{15}-1\}}$$

If there had been no period of four years to wait for sales then the formula would have been:

$$\frac{D}{S} = \frac{g(1+g)^{14}}{N\{(1+g)^{15}-1\}}$$

Taking a growth rate g of $0 \cdot 15$ (i.e. 15 per cent per annum) and assuming that after fifteen years of sales the expenditure on product development has settled down to 5 per cent of the sales, then we find that N has the value $5 \cdot 2$. Thus we find, on these assumptions that the cost of product development should not exceed 19 per cent of the annual sales which will be generated by the development. If it is unnecessary to wait four years before sales commence, then the cost may be as high as 33 per cent of the annual sales generated.

CONCLUSIONS

We may summarise the results of the calculations as follows:

If the cost of development is capitalised and the interest rate is $100p\%$, then the maximum permissible ratio of the cost of a development project to the annual sales resulting is given by:

$$\frac{\{1 - (1 - p)^{-15}\}f}{p(1 + p)^w}$$

where f is the fraction of the selling price that is set aside for the development cost and $(w + 1)$ is the number of years that elapse before the sales commence. This can usually be written as:

$$\frac{f}{p(1 + p)^w}$$

If the cost is absorbed as an expense in the year in which it is incurred, and the rate of growth is $100g\%$ per annum, then the maximum permissible ratio of the cost to the resulting annual sales is given by:

$$\frac{\{1 - (1 + g)^{15}\}f}{g(1 + g)^w}$$

which can usually be taken to be equal to:

$$\frac{f}{g(1 + g)^w}$$

The mathematical forms of the two expressions turn out to be identical, but in one case we use the rate of interest and in the other the rate of growth. In Appendix 3.2 it was suggested that it is good to set a minimum target for the profit at about 20 per cent on all assets used in the company. If we use the same criterion in product development, then we must charge interest at about 20 per cent. Since we are discussing long-term growth the tables given in Appendix 3.1 are relevant. For a small company that ploughs back most or all of its profits the maximum growth rate will be seen from the tables to be generally just a little less than the rate of profit on net assets. It follows that the two expressions lead, in practice, to similar results.

The practical conclusion that we have drawn for our business is that a product is usually worth developing if the annual sales can be expected to rise to about five times the total cost of the development programme.

4 Horizon Holidays

VLADIMIR RAITZ

My father was a doctor in Moscow and it was there that I was born in the year 1922 and lived during my early childhood. In 1928 my parents separated and my mother took me to Berlin and then to Poland. My mother and stepfather, who were living in Warsaw, thought that I might benefit from an English public school education and sent me off as a boarder at Mill Hill School in 1936. From there I went to the London School of Economics, which was evacuated to Cambridge during the war. I was not called up because I was then still a Soviet citizen, although I took British citizenship in 1949.

After graduating in 1943 I worked as a journalist, first with the United Press and later with Reuters. I was a journalist until 1949, when I hit upon the idea of the package holiday, and I have worked in this business ever since.

THE FIRST PACKAGE HOLIDAY

It was while I was on holiday at Calvi in Corsica that I had the idea of the package holiday. I had met some Russian friends who were just starting up in the holiday business and they asked me if I could get clients from England. At Calvi there was a holiday camp which consisted of tents, each of which had twin beds, and it was for this that I undertook to try to find English clients.

When I got back to London I had the problems of arranging cheap air travel to Calvi and then selling the holiday. The idea of low-cost charter flying had not been developed and I had quite a lot of difficulty arranging the charter of the aircraft.

Bureaucracies are proverbially distrustful of new ideas, and the Ministry of Civil Aviation in 1949 was no exception. The Ministry had no licensing machinery for people wanting to charter aircraft. However, I eventually obtained the Ministry's approval, and the company I had formed that year—Horizon Holidays Ltd—was granted a permit to operate in association with BEA. There were two chief restrictions. One was that there should be a minimum fare linked to the IATA air fare, and the other that the holiday should only be available to specified groups such as teachers, nurses and students.

With this licence I was able to tackle the problem of the charter of the aircraft. I negotiated the charter of a 32-seat DC-3 for fifteen return trips at £305 a trip, which of course works out at about £10 per person. I was able to finance the charter through a legacy of a little under £3,000 I had received from my grandmother a short while before.

The next problem was to advertise and attempt to sell the holiday. I put the first advertisements in the *Teachers World* and the *Nursing Mirror* in the spring of 1950. People who wrote in for further particulars were sent a duplicated brochure which gave the following information:

> 'Holidaymakers live in large tents fitted with beds and mattresses, two to a tent . . . the best sanitation . . . meals are taken out of doors . . . English visitors will be pleased to find that they are served twice daily with a meat dish . . . departures every Friday by Douglas DC-3 of Air Transport Charter (Channel Islands) Ltd . . . cost of this unique holiday is £35 10s.

At first I intended to run the holiday company as a part-time activity and keep on my journalism to provide me with an income. But I found after a few weeks that running the holiday business kept me pretty busy and I had to give up the journalism. I felt that I could easily get back into journalism if the holiday venture failed, and so the risk was not a particularly great one.

Our first year was disappointing. The sales of this package holiday did not go well and it only proved possible to sell

300 of the 480 seats I had chartered. This was not sufficient to cover the costs of the new venture. The chief reasons for the disappointing sales were probably that the advertising was placed too late in the year, and that I had priced the holiday too low and people just couldn't believe that a good holiday in Corsica could be had for the price quoted. But whatever the reason, the result was that I lost money on this first attempt.

However, I felt that the charter idea was sufficiently promising to be worth another try and I planned a second package holiday for 1951. My own finances were depleted by this time and I had to go to my bank manager to borrow for the next venture. I secured an overdraft for about £2,000 to finance the 1951 holidays. This time just over 400 holidays were sold. This took us over the break-even barrier and the company showed a profit for the year.

1952

In this year several developments took place. An airport had just been constructed at Palma in Majorca. I thought the Balearic Islands had great potential for tourist development and so wasted no time in making an application for a charter licence to the Air Transport Advisory Council. There were no direct air services to Majorca from London at this time and I was granted a licence for seven years for a weekly DC-3 flight. This negotiation added Majorca to Horizon's holiday programme.

In this year, 1952, we carried 700 holidaymakers and again the firm showed a profit. The company's profits were put back into the business and this has been my policy throughout the history of Horizon. No dividend has ever been declared. The retained profits have financed our expansion and we have never needed to borrow from the banks or elsewhere until about two years ago when large sums were required for hotel advances.

1953–1959

When a new business venture proves to be profitable it

inevitably happens that competitors enter the field, and this began to occur from 1953 onwards. Nevertheless, Horizon continued to expand, primarily because of our policy of ever seeking new ground. Every year we tried to open up a new centre for our clients that none of our competitors had developed: in 1954, Sardinia; in 1956, Perpignan for the Costa Brava, Malaga for the Costa del Sol, and Oporto in Portugal; in 1957, Minorca; in 1958, Tangier. The most successful of these was Perpignan, which was the airport in France serving Spain's Costa Brava, to which Horizon began to carry large numbers of British tourists in the middle and late 1950s. In 1959 we carried around 15,000 holiday-makers.

1959–1960

These years saw a temporary setback in the growth of the company. The competition of other operators became increasingly intense. This was partly because the introduction of the Viscount had so transformed BEA's economics that it was able in 1959 to extend the system of inclusive tour rebates by chopping the price to agents of seats on off-peak services to the point where they matched the seats on charter flights. This naturally gave us some serious competition.

In addition, there was a mushroom growth of get-rich-quick newcomers who managed to bypass the licensing procedure. The trick was to form phoney closed groups, and this led to a considerable diversion of clientele from the established tour organisers.

The result of these two sources of competition was that Horizon suffered a reduction in the number of holidays sold in 1960. But in 1961 and 1962 we recovered. This was due partly to a series of unfortunate experiences that many tourists suffered at the hands of the less reputable tour organisers about this time. In a number of incidents clients found that the holidays failed to live up to the promises made by the operators. On some occasions the hotels had not even been completed when the clients arrived. These disappointments were well publicised in the press and on radio and television and as a result the better established and reputable firms like Horizon gained increased custom.

But probably the most significant development at this time was the dramatic improvement in the facilities offered by charter operators, which in turn resulted from charter fleets in England and the Continent being transformed by the arrival of modern piston and turboprop aircraft which had been displaced from front-line schedule services by jets. Better aircraft meant increased competition and, once again, more competition led to a lowering and general stabilising of package holiday prices.

Horizon went into the sixties pretty confident that the inclusive tour was here to stay and very much aware that the surface of the travel market had, so far, only been scratched.

1961–1965

These years saw a continuous increase in the number of holidaymakers transported by Horizon. This increase is shown in Fig. 4.1. From 15,000 in 1959 the number of our clients grew steadily to 45,000 by 1965. Nevertheless, competition in these years was severe. One difficulty was that tour operators could get a licence virtually for the asking. There was increasing pressure to cut prices. Operators produced more and more extravagant brochures and improved the tours offered to sub-agents. The result was that profit margins were slim and to maintain them at all required increasing ingenuity.

The expansion of Horizon in this period was helped by the considerable growth in the demand for the package holiday. More and more people began to realise the economies of all-inclusive holidays by air. In the main, these were 'independent' travellers who had always made their own arrangements. Horizon benefited from this trend more than most companies because it had always respected most people's preference for 'individuality'. In the early days, the words 'inclusive tour' conjured up thoughts of a well-drilled squad of tourists being shepherded round in a sort of cultural obstacle-race with time off for organised relaxa-

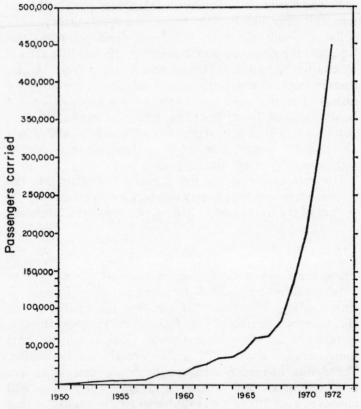

Figure 4.1   Growth of Horizon Group 1950–72

tion. But the picture soon changed, thanks largely to the original idea behind Horizon and the concept on which it was founded.

Horizon Holidays is based, and continues to exist, on the assumption that a certain sort of person doesn't need an organisation to tell him what to do; that he has the imagination to amuse himself and probably rather dislikes going round with a large ordered group; and that a representative is required to be on the spot, not to dragoon people into group activities, but simply to be there to provide help when needed.

This assumption has proved right. Horizon's overseas staff comprises approximately 200 representatives whose job is to know their areas like natives, to give help when required and, above all, not to be group cheer leaders.

1965-1972

Horizon has never felt the need to shed its role as 'pioneer'. New areas which the company has helped open up in the 1960s have given the British public a wider choice of resorts and centres in practically all the more popular Mediterranean countries: Tunisia, Portugal, Yugoslavia, Greece and many parts of Spain and Italy. In 1967, Horizon was one of the first to take advantage of the new licensing arrangements which resulted in significantly lower fares to Nairobi in Kenya, with the result that the vaste tourist potential of East Africa is at last beginning to be realised.

In 1970 Algeria made its debut together with the Costa Smeralda in Sardinia, Propriano in Corsica, Playa Esperanza in Majorca, Mojacar in Andalucia and Nerja on the Costa del Sol. Three air cruises to Russia were launched by Far Horizons, the company's long-haul division which became in 1969 the first major operator to market new low-price holidays in the Far East.

Both Horizon and Far Horizons continued to expand their programmes in 1971 with, among others, first-time arrangements to the Caribbean, the South Pacific and West Africa.

At the same time the company's first ever programme of Villa and Apartment holidays was launched.

For 1972 we offered a range of Mediterranean and Black Sea cruises on the Greek-owned *SS Phoenix*, reconverted to luxury standards. The ship is on exclusive charter to Horizon and has been redesigned to our own specifications.

TIME CHARTER METHODS

One of the more revolutionary developments has been the comparatively recent adoption by some tour operators—including Horizon—of 'time charter' methods. Here the tour operator buys a certain number of flying hours. This

G

new business relationship with airlines has significantly aided attempts to maintain low prices and has been a vital factor in the success of the package holiday industry. 'Time charter' involves a double risk. In the past, there was only one question-mark, relating to achievement of load factors. Today, the tour operator, having signed a 'time charter' agreement with an airline, is faced with the costly possibility of not reaching the stipulated minimum number of flying hours. Large organisations, like Horizon, are obviously better placed to guarantee flying hours to an airline; operators with less than 40,000 or 50,000 clients are of course in no position to enjoy the obvious benefits inherent in a 'time charter' agreement.

In recent years especially, the remarkably low prices which have appeared in holiday brochures have been due in great part to the achievement of 'time charter' targets. As with the load factor process, once the required minimum number of hours have been flown, the price per seat to the charterer is dramatically reduced. With year-round charter operations now the order of the day, low Winter Sunshine selling prices reflect the success of the previous summer's programme.

During the year ending November 1971, a three-year 'time charter' agreement, commencing in April 1972, was signed with British Caledonian, Europe's largest independent airline. At this point in time, the Horizon Group is the third largest tour operating company in the UK and will carry more than 350,000 holidaymakers during the summer 1972 season.

The Group's Winter Sunshine business has been growing at an even faster rate. In the 1971/2 off-peak season we shall have carried a little over 100,000 clients, compared with 55,000 during the previous winter.

As a Group, Horizon will be offering a capacity of more than 242,000 seats during the winter 1972/3 season—the largest off-season programme offered by any British tour operator.

SUBSIDIARY COMPANIES

During the 1960s Horizon established a number of subsidiaries and divisions to deal with different aspects of the business. In 1968, Horizon Midlands Ltd was set up to provide programmes of holidays based on direct flights from Birmingham, and, later, East Midland airports. Similarly, Horizon Holidays Scotland Ltd and Horizon Holidays (Ireland) Ltd were subsequently formed offering direct flight programmes from Glasgow and Dublin.

In 1966, we formed Club 18–30 to provide holidays for the younger age group. In 1968, Far Horizons was formed to provide holidays further afield than the Mediterranean. Our next subsidiary was Four S, which was set up to supply the lower end of the market. This was the first company to introduce the £10 weekend in Majorca, which was described by a leading trade newspaper as 'the most spectacular development on the inclusive tour scene for many years'. Four S was also the first operator to introduce an 'Instant Ticket' scheme which enables would-be travellers to walk into a travel agency and, minutes later, walk out with all the documents necessary for an inclusive air holiday. One travel agent described this new scheme as 'the most revolutionary idea since Cooks invented travellers' cheques'.

Horizon's own Late Bookings Service—'Zipticket'—has also proved to be a runaway success. A company survey, carried out in March 1972, showed that 81 per cent of travel agents considered 'Zipticket' the best service of its kind.

Later in 1969 we formed Four S Sports—a division specialising in inclusive charter arrangements for football supporters and other sporting enthusiasts. Four S Sports acts as official agent to such famous football clubs as Chelsea, Arsenal and Spurs and has also arranged trips abroad for motor racing, cricket and rugby fans. In 1971, Villas and Apartments was formed for selling Mediterranean villa and apartment holidays. In this year we also set up a Winter Sports division to provide winter ski holidays in Austria and Switzerland.

In addition, we have set up Horizon Travel branch offices in the centres of fourteen major towns throughout England and Wales, acting as general travel agencies as well as helping to sell the Group's services. But by far the greatest proportion (about 80 per cent) of Horizon holidays is sold through more than 1,500 appointed travel agents throughout the British Isles.

CONTROL OVER HOTELS

Another development has centred on our desire to obtain some control over the hotels to which our clients go. We have done this by leasing hotels for a term of years and installing our own managers. With such hotels under its control, the company is, of course, better placed to ensure higher all-round standards. At the same time, a drop in service efficiency is that much more easily put right.

In 1971, the Horizon Group managed a total of ten hotels in the Mediterranean area: the Hotels Torremora, Costa del Sol and Marymar in Torremolinos; Grand Hotel Las Forcas in San Feliu; Club El Catalan, Estartit; Hotel Fenicia, Benidorm; Hotel Entremare, La Manga; Hotel Mojacar, Mojacar; Hotel Isabela, Santa Ponsa (Four S Travel); Hotel Lord Nelson, Playa de Santo Tomas. In addition, the group has bought the freeholds of two other hotels.

Anticipating our future hotel requirements abroad, Horizon Holiday Developments (International) Ltd was formed recently. Owned jointly by Associated Development Holdings Ltd and ourselves, the company is concerned with the development of hotel and villa accommodation abroad to be featured in future Horizon programmes.

COMPUTERISATION, NEW PREMISES, PERSONNEL POLICIES

In September 1969, to cope with our rapid expansion, an ICL 1901A computer was installed at Horizon's head office in Hanover Street in the West End of London. The computer is programmed to carry out a number of important functions hitherto dealt with manually or by a tabulator system. These include the pricing of holidays, the processing and accounting of bookings and the production of hotel rooming lists and flight manifests. The computer also provides management, on a regular basis, with vital information on a variety of subjects, including a detailed analysis of bookings taken. It has recently been programmed to produce an integrated financial and costing system and original typeset matter to facilitate brochure production.

In April 1972, the computer and the department responsible for it have been moved to new premises leased by Horizon at Acton, West London. Other departments now based at these new offices include reservations, accounts and personnel. The directors of the company, its Continental, aircraft planning, public relations, brochure production and sales departments have remained at Hanover Street. Horizon Holidays also has three provincial offices in Manchester, Cardiff and Newcastle, the latter two being shared with Horizon Travel.

I have always thought it important to keep the staff of the company happy and well motivated. We endeavour to encourage long-term loyalty to the company by increasing benefits in accordance with length of service. Holidays and sick pay are raised with the number of years our staff have worked with the company. Salaries are raised automatically once a year to take account of the increase in the cost of living over the period. In addition, each department head submits an evaluation once a year of the staff in his department and on the basis of these further salary increases may be awarded.

RECENT PROFITS AND GROWTH

The following summary of the number of holidays sold in the period since 1968, split between the two seasons, gives an indication of the way in which the Group's operations have grown:

Winter		Summer	
1967/8	6,000	1968	78,000
1968/9	14,000	1969	122,000
1969/70	23,000	1970	178,000
1970/1	55,000	1971	260,000
1971/2	101,000	1972	350,000 (approx.)

Record Group profits of £600,000 (pre-tax) achieved in 1969 were reduced the following year mainly as a result of high development costs incurred in pursuing new ventures overseas and establishing specialist subsidiary companies and divisions at home. The profits of the four principal companies in the Group for 1970 were as follows:

Horizon Holidays	£110,000
Horizon Travel	50,000
Horizon Midlands	100,000
Horizon Scotland	30,000
	£290,000

The value of the company is of course difficult to assess, but in 1971 a figure of £5 million was suggested. In *The Times 1,000* list of major companies in the western world for 1971, Horizon is placed in rank 981 for capital value and eighth in terms of profitability as a percentage of capital value. This percentage is given as 76·1 per cent.

Horizon Midlands Ltd, in particular, has achieved an excellent growth and profits record, with the result that the company was 'floated' in May 1972. It is the first independent package holiday company ever to come to market. The 'offer for sale'—1,760,000 ordinary shares of 5p each at 70p per share—was oversubscribed 8·7 times.

Horizon Midlands' first year of operation proved to be a virtual sell-out; it was one of the very few tour operators to have made a profit in its first year.

The following is a summary of the number of holidays sold by Horizon Midlands since its formation:

Summer		Winter	
1966	5,000		
1967	6,400		
1968	5,900	1968–9	1,300
1969	21,500	1969–70	2,600
1970	35,300	1970–1	13,600
1971	61,800	1971–2	32,600

Horizon Midlands was the first provincial tour operator to have its own time charter agreement—a Boeing 737 jet of Britannia Airways from 1 March 1970 to 31 March 1974.

The company now handles nearly half of all the inclusive tour traffic through Birmingham and East Midland airports, which themselves are securing an increasingly dominant share of the traffic generated in their surrounding areas.

Following the share offer, Horizon Holidays' holding in Horizon Midlands has been reduced to a little under 53 per cent.

Horizon Midlands' profits before taxation for the year ending 30 November 1971 increased to £284,000, while profits for 1972 are being forecasted as being 'not less than £390,000'.

HORIZON'S REPUTATION

In an exceptionally competitive business like our own, the company's reputation is of considerable importance. We take a close interest in how holidaymakers view different holiday operators and in particular in the reputation of Horizon. Accordingly, in 1968 we asked an independent market research organisation to carry out an enquiry among a representative sample of travel agents throughout the country to ascertain the agents' views on the services provided by all leading tour operators. Our object was to see how we stood so that we would be able to find out any weak points in our services to our clients, which we should then be able to put right.

The questions put to the agents were as follows:

1. Which company is most likely to provide accommodation of a high standard?
2. Which company is most likely to give satisfaction to customers and attract few complaints?
3. Which company is the most experienced in the air charter holiday business?
4. Which company has the most informative brochure?
5. Which company is most likely to have a wide choice of resorts?
6. Which company would you recommend to your most experienced and discerning clients?

7. Which company would you choose for your *own* holiday?

The result of this survey showed that Horizon was the first choice of the agents in their answers to all seven questions. This was of course a gratifying conclusion. We have commissioned similar surveys each year since 1968—the most recent was carried out by National Opinion Polls—and have kept the leading place annually. In the latest survey, carried out in April 1972, Horizon again came first in reply to each of the questions asked, scoring almost three times as many points as the runner-up.

We shall strive to retain this position in the years to come. In our business, as in others, it is fatal not to keep in touch with the needs of your customers.

Perhaps it may seem that the growth of Horizon has been smooth and effortless. This is not the case and the development of the company has required constant attention and effort. In a business of this kind there are continual crises of one sort or another over which we have little or no control, that have to be sorted out. This is one of our major problems. In addition, we have had to be constantly on the look out for new holiday locations. And again, the holiday industry is exceptionally competitive, the profit margins are low and we have to be careful to keep costs down in every part of our operations. Perhaps we have been lucky that we have not encountered any major setback, except for our first year. But this has not been accomplished without considerable attention to detail.

5 Ryans Tourist Holdings

DERMOT A. RYAN

I have heard an entrepreneur defined as 'a man whose major source of satisfaction in life is in meeting challenges, finding challenging tasks and doing a good job at overcoming them. This is where the entrepreneur gets his pleasure in life.' The term 'entrepreneur' is most frequently used to describe a successful businessman, but I find this an oversimplification. A better definition might be one who is not prepared to let fate come to him but rather goes out to seek it.

It must be appreciated that a true entrepreneur need not necessarily be a good organiser, manager or administrator, and in fact the real entrepreneur may very well fail to shine in any of these areas. Entrepreneurial success springs rather from a mind that is never satisfied, and so it follows that interest wanes once a project is launched. I propose to let the reader judge to what extent these definitions of entre-preneurial activity are supported by the history and develop-ment of the undertaking for which I am responsible. I will start therefore with a description of my businesses.

On completion of my secondary education I entered university and in 1949, whilst studying for a degree in economics at University College, Dublin, I bought a half share in a 1935 Ford 10 car. This was hired out at £10 per week and at the end of a year we had made £80 profit. We then sold the car for £80 and thus recovered our entire original outlay.

That was my most successful investment ever, realising a clear 100 per cent profit in a year. The confidence I gained from this success led me to buy my own second-hand car. Perhaps I believed Mark Twain's saying 'All you need in this life is ignorance and confidence, then success is sure', but I must have been lacking in either ignorance or confidence or both because the venture was a complete disaster. The car had so many faults that after two hirings I decided to get rid of it and to cut my losses. Ten days after purchasing it, I resold it at a loss of £22 10s. This was a classic example of success leading to overconfidence and it left me slightly shaken and questioning the validity of Mark Twain's 'ignorance'.

You may well wonder why a project which lost £22 10s is mentioned in a book on 'the entrepreneur' but I think it is worth inclusion if only to make the point that an entrepreneur has no insurance against failure. If a setback disqualifies one from being an entrepreneur then I am disqualified, and that more than once.

EARLY DEVELOPMENT

I exercised more care in the purchase of my next car and, as a result, soon made up my losses.

It quickly became apparent to me that the demand for car hire exceeded the supply and I decided to expand. Since my own capital was limited, I approached the usual channels and found my bank manager surprisingly sympathetic to one so young, and our good relationship continued through the years until his retirement last year. I have never changed my bank and have never forgotten their confidence in me. As a result of the success of this approach I soon had a fleet of six cars on the road and business was thriving.

LEARNING MY BUSINESS

I was now a university graduate with a BA degree in economics and a fleet owner employing six people. I recognised at this stage the tremendous importance of establishing competitive advantage over rival companies and became aware of my own lack of knowledge of the car hire business. I wrote to a large care hire firm in London, offering to work for them for nothing, and they accepted. I spent three weeks as unpaid receptionist, dealing with reservations, filling in forms and studying systems and procedures. I then became a mechanics assistant; studying garage procedures and systems generally.

DELEGATION

The need to leave my business in another's hands while I was in London compelled me to delegate and I decided that, in my case at least, it would not be something negative but an aggressive move to secure the benefits of direct and immediate decision making. I delegated the responsibility for my business and, with it, full authority.

I am convinced that proper delegation—that is, giving authority to equal responsibility—is the essence of business management and administration. Apart from its greater organisational flexibility, such delegation creates much more commitment and consequently gives greater job satisfaction.

FIRST DIVERSIFICATION

The car hire fleet grew with the post-war growth in tourist business and I began to question the wisdom of using only second-hand cars for the fleet. I felt that these were not the best for car hire business and decided to convert to a fleet of new cars which would be replaced each year by more new cars. The current year's fleet could be sold in bulk, but rather than do this through some garage I decided to enter the car sales business myself. Thus my first diversification arose more from a change within my existing business than from a desire to capture new peaks.

An organisation was established to dispose of the car hire fleet at the end of each season and proved quite satisfactory.

RYANS RADIO CABS

Dublin's taxi service in the 1950s was probably comparable to that of any other city with a population of 650,000, but it seemed rather obvious that it suffered from a serious communications problem. I felt that the idea of a radio taxi service was a good one and Ryans Radio Cabs was launched in November 1957.

At first it was the centre of what subsequently became known as 'the taxi war'. The 'war' caused Ryan's Radio Cabs to travel hundreds of thousands of miles to pick up non-existent passengers, and at one stage it was losing almost £6,000 per month. A variation in the 'war' came when acid was thrown on a Rolls Royce which was being operated as a taxi. Another taxi—a Morris Cowley—was found completely burnt out on the outskirts of Dublin having been hijacked at gunpoint in the best current aeroplane fashion. The driver, fortunately, had been evicted at an earlier stage.

We weathered the storm, however, and soon were considering a change of approach which would involve the drivers much more immediately in the running of the business and would introduce, in a very practical way, the concept of industrial democracy.

This new plan was to appoint owner drivers to the fleet who would retain the fares paid and could employ co-drivers if necessary. They paid their own road tax, petrol, insurance and the many other sundry items which are a part of car ownership. They also paid Ryans a weekly rental to supply them with business from our centrally controlled radio station. Our costs were therefore greatly reduced since we provided only the radio and illuminated signs for car roofs, staffing and equipment for the radio base station, together with advertising promotion, and collection of accounts which were kept to a minimum.

This system changed the business into a profit-making one although nowadays it is a small part of our overall business.

PETROL SALES

Entrepreneurism is rarely just a single stroke, but rather a single idea from which an enterprise is started. By the time the idea comes to fruition it has been modified and altered and gradually built into the business or service which eventually emerges. The nearest example to the one-stroke success concerns the petrol business.

Broadly speaking, petrol retailing in Ireland is not a very profitable business. A profusion of petrol stations exists and it is not uncommon to meet with four or five stations on a one-mile stretch of road. With a smaller volume of traffic compared to many other countries, this leads to small turnover and consequently small profits. In provincial areas many of the petrol pumps are attached to shops or public houses and are run as sidelines.

In 1960 we had only one petrol station which was attached to our self-drive garage in Dublin. It produced a large turnover because, apart from passing traffic, it was also used to fill all the self-drive cars before they were given out on hire. Consequently, it was a worthwhile account for a petrol company.

The normal dealership system gives the retailer a mark-up and then a further rebate on volume of $0 \cdot 156p$ which is normally paid yearly in arrears. Following an enquiry by the Fair Trade Commission into Solus petrol stations—which were tied to selling one brand of petrol over a long period of years—a new order was being introduced which would not allow such agreements to continue for more than five years. We were negotiating around this time with Esso for a new agreement and on the day before the new order was to come into operation we sat around a table at 11.00 a.m. and remained there for $19\frac{1}{2}$ hours, at the end of which time a new twenty-year agreement was finally signed. This agreement incorporated an arrangement whereby we would receive a rebate in advance instead of in arrears.

In other words, if, at the end of the first two-year period, we were selling 5,000 gallons of petrol per week on average, we would receive a rebate—which was then $1\frac{3}{4}$ old pence per gallon—multiplied by 52 and multiplied by 18, representing the balance of the twenty-year agreement period. We would, of course, also receive the extra rebate on the increased volume actually achieved during those two years, as well as receiving the rebate in advance, on the assumption that we would maintain that volume for the coming eighteen years.

If, at the end of the next two-year period, our gallonage

further increased, we would then receive the additional weekly gallonage multiplied by 52 multiplied by 16, representing the remaining years of the agreement, and so on over the twenty years. Conversely, of course, if our gallonage dropped at the end of any two-year period we would have to repay an amount equal to the drop in volume multiplied by 52 and multiplied by the remaining number of years. This has never occurred and we are now in the eleventh year of the agreement.

Taken on a discounted cash-flow basis this is quite a remarkable agreement and I am led to believe that the deal is unique, anywhere in the world. At the time it was signed nobody, not even ourselves, quite realised its potential, but shortly afterwards when we had time to assess its true potential we bought another petrol station with a view to increasing gallonage, thereby getting a large amount of working capital which would be available to plough back into any part of the business.

Since 1962 we have, in fact, received £272,369 in advance rebates, and we now have nine petrol stations in Dublin city and county.

CARAVANS

We had recognised for some time that the car hire business was only one part of the tourist market, and while the concept of the 'package holiday' was still quite new the question of holiday accommodation had frequently been in our minds.

Accommodation suggested hotels and, while Ryan Hotels possibly first entered my mind around this time, we were aware that capital costs would be very heavy and that the return on investment initially would be slow. We were not happy to drop the question of accommodation entirely and decided 'If not hotels, then why not caravans?'. This further diversification into caravans was accomplished in 1962 by taking over three existing seaside caravan resorts at Kilkee (Co. Clare), Bettystown (Co. Meath) and Salthill (Galway). The three resorts are now on well-developed sites with toilet and shower facilities, laundry rooms, TV rooms and games rooms.

There is a resident manager in each resort and at peak summer season there are almost 400 caravans in use.

Caravans are replaced after the second or third seasons and our carsales division is the outlet for selling them, although many are bought and collected from the site.

The caravan section is important and will become more important as this type of holiday accommodation increases in popularity.

TRAVEL AGENCY

During the continued growth of our car hire business, bookings were handled by a special section of our staff. This section also looked after caravan bookings but in 1969, shortly after the acquisition of the three caravan resorts, we acquired a travel agency with offices in Middle Abbey Street, and the booking section was transferred there.

Renamed 'Ryans Travel Agency', this latest acquisition was a logical development and the timing was determined by the increasing pressure and volume of bookings being dealt with in our booking office. It also placed Ryans in the travel business for Irish and foreign holidays, both incoming and outgoing. There are now Ryan travel offices also in London and New York.

PUBLIC COMPANY

In 1964, Ryans became a public company with 1,960,000 ordinary shares of 1s each offered for sale at 3s 3d per share. At this stage activities included car hire, caravan holidays, car sales, radio taxis and petrol sales. The Group's combined annual profits had risen from £6,237 in 1960 to £59,798 in the year ended 31 August 1964.

Our management team was probably the youngest of any Irish public company. I was chairman aged thirty-five, and our managing director was aged thirty-two, while the next four in line of management authority were aged from thirty to thirty-five. This young management team had brought the company to a situation where our fixed assets, after depreciation, amounted to £486,671 while our current assets amounted to £339,181.

MANAGEMENT

I have already mentioned my views on delegation, and experience has strengthened rather than weakened my view that delegation is the essence of management—that is, delegation designed to seek all the benefits of instant decision making by pushing responsibility and authority as far down the line as possible.

In Ryans, delegation is an aggressive and positive move and is in no way a negative response to the needs of overburdened and overworked senior executives. This kind of delegation makes for greater organisational flexibility and drive, and one other major benefit is that it undeniably gives a very much higher degree of job satisfaction. Strong lines of communication have always been, and still are, maintained throughout the company. Modern budgeting and accounting methods are in operation and each division produces its own annual forecasts which are deliberately kept flexible.

In addition to the managing director there is an assistant managing director (finance) and an assistant managing director (marketing). Each division of Ryans also has a divisional general manager.

FURTHER DIVERSIFICATION

The pace of business, as in life generally, seems to be constantly accelerating and the number of diversifications and mergers very great. Nothing in business is permament or constant, but whilst diversification was still very much in our thoughts, we felt quite strongly that we should concern ourselves, at this stage at least, with developments or diversifications in tourism. This train of thought led logically to accommodation and, ultimately, back to hotels.

HOTELS

At that time—the mid-sixties—the hotel industry in Ireland offered many attractions, including substantial grants and considerable tax advantages. In order to encourage the much-needed provision of further accommodation Bord Failte—the Irish tourist body—offered grants for the building of hotel bedrooms. In addition to these, the cost of hotels could be written off against profits tax free over a period of ten years. Despite these benefits, however, the hotel industry is so highly capital intensive that no decision was made until more than two years had been spent on investigation, market research and planning.

After much soul searching, the decision was finally taken to enter the hotel industry and a site was purchased in Killarney. We announced publicly a plan to build 800 rooms in 5 years. Our original plan envisaged a 60 bedroomed motel-style hotel on the Killarney site and building operations commenced in September 1967.

In November 1967 an existing hotel on eight acres near Shannon Airport became available. We examined this thoroughly and it was purchased thus becoming the second Ryan hotel. Plans were drawn up fairly soon to enlarge this existing 30 bedroomed hotel to a 90 bedroomed hotel.

Our developing interest in hotels became widely known at this stage and we received many offers of existing hotels and of suitable sites as a result of which a site was purchased at Galway and an hotel in Sligo. Between April 1968 and September 1969 four hotels were opened: Killarney Ryan Hotel in April 1968; Limerick Ryan Hotel in July 1968; Galway Ryan Hotel in May 1969; and Yeats County Ryan Hotel (Sligo) in September 1969.

LONDON RYAN HOTEL

Our fifth hotel—the London Ryan Hotel—opened in King's Cross in June 1972. Six storeys high and with 450 beds, it cost just over £1 million. As building operations had commenced before 1 April 1971 we qualified for English Tourist Board grants amounting to £200,000.

H

At first glance, one might form the impression that the decision to open the London hotel was an ad hoc venture, but nothing could be further from the truth. Neither were we unduly influenced by the fact that we would be the first Irish hotel company to build a hotel in London. The decision was a hard-headed business one, following almost two years of extensive market research which turned up much interesting data, for instance a well-based estimate that before 1975 the demand for London hotel bed nights would have exceeded 20 million. But more important from our point of view was the fact that for every one US visitor who came to Ireland at that time, five would go to London. Research also indicated that the average US tourist wished to spend only five days in Ireland, so it seemed to us quite clear that an inclusive package holiday incorporating both Britain and Ireland would be a major selling factor in North America and indeed on the Continental market as well.

This ability to sell London would of course benefit the company's Irish hotels, making it possible to sell package holidays, including Ireland, to people who would otherwise not have visited this country at all. While the London Ryan Hotel represents our first hotel outside Ireland, we intend to continue this programme of development in the future.

TOUR OPERATORS

The emphasis on clearly defined sections of the business such as car hire, petrol, taxis and hotels may have tended to obscure Ryan's growth as tour operators. We are in fact the largest independent tour operator in Ireland selling to the world markets with particular emphasis on Great Britain, North America and Europe and, of course, to the Irish market itself. Our 'Go as you please' touring holidays using any one of our four Irish hotels have been immensely successful in this age of the mobile tourist. The London Ryan Hotel has enabled us to sell an Ireland/Britain holiday. We use Ryans hotels where possible, but we also use other hotels where necessary for our tours, which are constantly changed and modified in response to market trends.

FURTHER DEVELOPMENT

Whatever success we achieved was much more attributable to the team of managers than to myself. Their administrative capability has been of the greatest importance. Management training is valued by all of us and in order to keep abreast of new managerial methods and techniques I spent a year at Stanford University in California, following the course for Master of Business Administration. It spoke highly for the work done by the management team within the company that I should be the first Irishman admitted to the Sloan Group for this degree and also the first executive from a company with assets of less than $100 million to qualify for the fellowship.

The entrepreneur must constantly and continuously study his market and his competitors, but more importantly, he must seek out new management techniques and make his mind receptive to new ideas. I have given an account, so far, of the tourist business but I suppose I could say that new thinking led to my acquisition in 1969 of a very old-established and well-known company in the automative and electrical distributive field—Traders Magneto and Dynamo Co. Ltd.

TRADERS MAGNETO AND DYNAMO CO. LTD

This company was founded in 1926 as an auto-electrical workshop and is now one of the largest companies in Ireland in the automative and electrical components and accessories field, employing 100 staff. The company has continued its expansion, and between 1969 and 1971 new branches were opened in Athlone and Limerick and more modern and extensive premises were acquired in Cork.

Amongst the many exclusive agencies held by Traders Magneto and Dynamo Co. Ltd are Vent Axia, the pioneers of ventilation equipment, and Armstrongs, who are the largest non-American manufacturers of shock absorbers in the world.

Profits in Traders Magneto and Dynamo Co. Ltd had

grown from £6,872 in 1966 to £48,500 in 1970, at which stage it was decided to seek a quotation from the Irish Stock Exchange. A new public company—Ryan-Traders Distribution Ltd—was floated in September 1971 and the offer was oversubscribed eleven times.

Ryan-Traders Distribution Ltd was the first public issue on the Irish Stock Exchange for more than two years, and in introducing the issue to the public, the company announced that one of its primary purposes would be to diversify through acquisition.

In a very short time we had acquired Robin Rennicks Ltd, a Dublin company engaged in tyre distribution, remoulding and importing, who had the exclusive agency for Yokohama tyres. In early 1972, Ensign Accumulators Ltd in London, makers and distributors of Ensign batteries, was acquired.

Ryan-Traders Distribution Ltd is still actively interested in, and pursuing, many other prospective lines of development. Our management philosophy is obviously the same as that which proved successful with Ryans Tourist Holdings Ltd, and while the two companies are completely independent, there are very close links.

STAFF RELATIONS

Active communication at all levels are encouraged in both Ryans Tourist Holdings Ltd and Ryan-Traders Distribution Ltd. A staff magazine, *Ryans Review*, is published quarterly. On the acquisition of Traders Magneto and Dynamo Co. Ltd, a special staff magazine, *Traders Times*, was introduced.

THE ROLE OF THE ENTREPRENEUR

Our world of today is a very different place from the world of a hundred or even fifty years ago, mainly because of the entrepreneurial activities of our forebears. If entrepreneurs had not developed new concepts, new philosophies and new products we would be still living in a primitive age with stone houses and perhaps wooden ploughshares.

Our society of today is built on the successes of men such

as Henry Ford who pioneeered a new method of transport, the Wright brothers who gave man wings, Edison, Alexander Graham Bell, and Christopher Columbus whose voyage to America anticipated our present space exploration programme.

Some may consider the entrepreneur to be concerned solely with his own advancement and not with the good of society, but this is a distorted concept. Justifiably, he gains profit or satisfaction, or both, but the real beneficiary is society itself which gains either a product or a service or a concept which would not otherwise be available. Henry Ford may have made millions from the old 'tin lizzie' but each succeeding generation has gained more and more from his then revolutionary idea of providing the people with cheap and reliable transport.

The true entrepreneur may well become a big businessman, but size is hardly the main criterion for deserving the name entrepreneur. Growth may be circumscribed by various conditions, and circumstances at a particular time may be completely unfavourable. Many entrepreneurs are probably little known outside their own immediate environment, but their activities are nonetheless entrepreneurial.

CONCLUSION

An old Chinese proverb, 'What is the use of running when you are on the wrong road?', is a very useful guide and warning to the entrepreneur. By all means run—when you are on the right road!

6 Turkey Culture

BERNARD T. MATTHEWS

I was born on the Norfolk/Suffolk borders. Except for holidays, and my national service in the Royal Air Force, I have lived in Norfolk for the whole of my life. My father was a working-class man who changed his job on many occasions. In consequence, my family moved house frequently, and I therefore attended a number of schools before I was ten years old. At some of the schools I was successful, at others, where I attended for only short periods, I was far from successful. My strongest subject at primary school was mental arithmetic, and I was often admonished for shouting out the answer to a question before anyone else in the class had time to answer! At my last primary school I passed the eleven-plus examination and won a place to the local grammar school in Norwich.

My education at the local grammar school can hardly be called a great success. Having started in the top stream at the age of eleven, over the next five years I gradually made my way down to the bottom stream, and was finally asked to leave by the headmaster in my fifth year because it was considered a waste of time for me to take the Cambridge School Certificate examination.

My first job on leaving school was with a firm of livestock auctioneers, at a salary of 32s 6d per week. I had always been interested in livestock and had spent most of my school holidays whilst at the grammar school on my brother-in-law's farm, where I worked to earn pocket money to pay for my clothes and also to buy such things as bicycles etc.

To make additional money, I started running a small dance band in which I played the drums. I mention this

because it led to a very important event in my life. At one of
the dances at which my band was playing I met my future
wife, who was to play such an important part in the development of Bernard Matthews Ltd at a later date.

Having worked for the firm of auctioneers for two years,
I was conscripted into the Royal Air Force for my national
service, where I stayed until the age of twenty. On returning
from the RAF in April 1950, I returned to my job as an
auctioneer's clerk, and my salary was increased by 5s per
week to the princely sum of 37s 6d per week! It was obvious
to me that I had to earn some additional pocket money from
somewhere in order to try and save money, because at this
level of wage, with bus fares etc., at the end of each week I
had very little money left.

After I had returned to the auctioneering firm for about
one month, in one of the auction markets which I attended
on Thursdays twenty turkey eggs were offered, which I
purchased for one shilling each; and on the same day a
paraffin oil incubator was offered, which I purchased for
£1 10s. At that time the only capital I had in the world was
the £2 10s which I had now expended on the turkey eggs
and the incubator. I carried the eggs home on the bus that
night, and arranged for the small incubator to be brought
home by a friend of mine in the back of his van. The incubator was set up in the garden shed at my mother-in-law's
house in the village of Taverham. At this time I was lodging
with my wife's mother, as my own parents had divorced and
were living in London.

From the twenty turkey eggs I hatched twelve turkeys,
and by saving a few shillings each week from my salary, I
managed to feed the birds until they were four weeks old.
At this stage I sold them to a local farmer for 15s each. The
mortality had been nil, and therefore for my original investment of £2 10s I had already had a turnover of £9, the vast
majority of which was profit.

I now changed my job by joining the branch office of a
large national insurance company as a clerk. My main
reason for the change of job was that I was offered a salary
with the insurance company at twice the level which I was

earning in the auctioneering business. Having made a small profit, but a high return on capital employed, I started to make my plans for 1951. As my capital was very restricted, I decided to try and find farmers who had flocks of breeding turkeys and to purchase eggs from them, using my capital to buy additional small incubators. During 1951 I purchased some half-dozen paraffin incubators, each of which would hold about sixty turkey eggs; and I then made contracts with three or four local farmers to purchase eggs from them in the season. At this time the turkey business was totally seasonal, and the turkeys started to lay eggs naturally about the first week in April, and continued to lay until about the first week in July.

I started to advertise the day-old turkey poults in the local paper, and found that there was a ready demand for them. I had no difficulty in selling all I produced at something like 6s each for day-olds, whilst I was able to purchase the eggs at 2s 6d each; and by hatching approximately two out of three eggs placed in the incubators, I had a chick cost which was slightly in excess of 4s, so that on each of the birds which I sold I was earning 2s profit.

In 1952 I adopted the same policy, purchasing more incubators: by this time they had reached some twenty in number; and making further contracts with local farmers and hatching turkeys during the natural season. Again I was able to sell all I produced, and decided at this point—having accumulated some capital and hired a further 10 acres of land at the back of my mother-in-law's house—that I would keep a flock of breeding turkeys for myself. My wife had already given up her job as secretary to a local builder, and she was now spending the whole of her time in looking after our rather antiquated but quite successful hatchery.

During the autumn and winter of 1952–3 I worked for the insurance company from 9 to 5, and worked for myself from 6 to 8 in the mornings and from 6·30 to midnight in the evenings, and all day Saturday and Sunday. During this period, with my limited capital, I had to find the very cheapest building materials available, because the only thing I had in abundance was my own time! From these very cheap materials, by tarring and waterproofing, I built some brooding units and turkey-rearing houses and set up pens across the 10-acre field to keep my first 100 breeding turkeys.

In August 1952 my wife and I were married, and because we already had some of the turkeys growing, our honeymoon was limited to a period from Saturday afternoon until Monday morning—for we had to return to feed the turkeys!

Having constructed all the pens and the houses for the breeding turkeys, there was now so much work that I decided that the time had come for me to enter the turkey business on a full-time basis, and I therefore gave notice to the Commercial Union Assurance Co. Ltd. I left them on the last Friday in January 1953, and on the Saturday night there was a great storm on the east coast, during which many people lost their lives due to flooding etc. The effect on me was that all the houses and pens I had worked so hard on for the previous six to nine months were blown over, and all the turkeys which had been in the rearing pens escaped. When I got up to begin work early on Sunday morning, there was not a turkey in sight! My turkeys had heard some male turkeys some 2 miles away and had made their way towards these birds. I caught the turkeys and brought them back and set up the pens once again, and started to breed the turkeys.

The first season was not very successful, as we had by this time collected together some extremely heavy types of turkey, for which natural mating was almost impossible. So we had to develop a method of artificial insemination. We were probably, even on our small scale, the first people to breed turkeys by artificial methods commercially in the United Kingdom.

In 1954 we decided to rear some 5,000 turkeys for Christmas out of the profits which had been accumulating from selling day-old turkey chicks to other farmers; but by this time we were expanding at a very fast rate but were not controlling the business properly; and during the year we experienced a fair amount of disease among the birds. We found that we had a most unprofitable year. However, we didn't stop—we expanded again in 1955; this time we had a most successful year and by then had outgrown the facilities available to us.

I started to look around for new premises, and one type of property in particular—a large mansion, which at that time were selling for very low prices in the country of Norfolk due to the cost of upkeep. I found such a place in the form of Great Witchingham Hall, a large mansion of Tudor origins with Victorian additions, which I purchased, together with 36 acres of land, for a total sum of £3,000. I managed to obtain a mortgage from one of my customer friends for £2,500, so my total investment at this point in the new premises was £500.

In the beginning we lived and operated the office side of the business in one room in the mansion, whilst we slept in another room. At the same time we started to build brooder equipment for young turkeys which we placed in the thirty bedrooms of the mansion. In what had been the dining room we placed large electric incubators and started to produce some 2–3,000 turkeys per week during the season, the vast majority of these still being sold to local farmers either as day-old or four-week-old turkeys.

By the end of 1955 we had committed ourselves with every pound's worth of capital that we had been able to lay our hands on. We had a bank overdraft of £3,000 and liabilities from feed compounders for over six months of our total turnover.

As so often happens when a business is expanding at too fast a rate, we did not have a very profitable year in 1956. We started off with a poor hatching season, because many of the sheds for the greatly expanded production were not ready on time, and we did not have enough management at that time to control the 300 per cent increase in production that we were then involved with. Even so, we made profits during the hatching season, but by this time we were growing significant numbers of turkeys for the Christmas market. Very few statistics were available concerning the total turkey industry, and I did not know that other people within the industry were also expanding at a very fast rate. When we came to sell the turkeys in the autumn we found that instead of receiving 4s 6d per lb as we had in 1955, the market became more and more depressed until during November we were receiving 1s 9d per lb. for large 20 lb. turkeys, plucked and delivered to the Smithfield market. Although we did not know what our production costs were at that time exactly, we certainly knew that they were in excess of 1s 9d per lb.! The fact was that at this selling price we were losing money on a considerable scale.

Although there had been a 100 per cent increase in production and heavily reduced prices, the increased production was being consumed, and during 1956 a 100 per cent increase in consumption of turkeys in the United Kingdom at Christmas time had occurred.

During 1956 we had started to process frozen, oven-ready turkeys for the first time. These were killed, dressed and packed in what were the kitchens of the mansion, and were then delivered twice a day by me some 30 to 40 miles to a freezing company who had a large cold store, where the birds were frozen, and I would travel back the next day to put them into cardboard boxes. Because of the very depressed market we found it difficult, if not impossible, to sell what was a comparatively new product while the total industry was receiving very low prices for its conventional product, i.e. the fresh turkey.

So the birds concerned were left in store; they amounted to some 3,000 birds, and it was not until Boxing Day when I read the national newspapers I discovered that due to the very low prices there had been an enormous demand for turkeys that Christmas, and the situation had finished up on Christmas Eve without a turkey available anywhere in the country. I was therefore able, two days after Christmas, to sell my first oven-ready turkeys at a price of 5s 6d per lb. for the New Year trade in Scotland.

Even though I had sold the 3,000 birds at a good price I was left in a very difficult financial position. By this time our creditors were equivalent to the whole of the previous year's turnover and we were finding it very, very difficult indeed even to obtain further feed credit. However, we had a further 100 per cent increase in breeding stock and we had an order book full as far as the sale of day-old turkeys was concerned. Although things looked black at this point, they did not look impossible.

On a Monday morning during February a blizzard started to blow at about 8 a.m. with heavy snow. The snow started to freeze on the electricity lines and about two hours later we ceased to have an electricity supply, due to the main cables falling down. The incubators were full of eggs and we had a full order book for turkey chicks. We waited during the day, hoping that the power would be restored, but the blizzard continued and by mid-afternoon most of the roads had been closed by snowdrifts, and we were unable to travel by motor vehicle from Great Witchingham at all. Some of our staff were also marooned with us, and we just did not know what to do. My wife had made her way to the village to buy as many oil lamps as possible in order to keep the birds which had already hatched alive, and we allowed the birds to run across the floors of the rooms and used the hot water pipes of our antiquated central heating system to help bolster up the temperature.

I knew that providing we had the current restored within twelve hours or so, because of the insulation and the heat generated by the eggs in the incubators we should have few problems with the hatch. As I sat on that Monday evening, with no electricity anywhere, and had my evening meal by candlelight, I started to wonder what would happen if the power was not restored. It was not restored by 10 o'clock, and we were then told by the Electricity Board that it would be virtually impossible for them to restore the power for several days. I arrived at the point where I almost gave up any hope of continuing in business.

I was extremely depressed for an hour or so, and could see that if I did not hatch the eggs which were in the incubators, then I had no chance of survival with such a bad financial position on my hands. I started to think how I could possibly get over the problems which were confronting me. An idea came to me. The central heating system of the house was still operating, although the water was not being pumped completely round the house because the electricity controlling the pumps was not working. But there was a supply of hot water close to the incubators. I tapped the central heating system with an ordinary garden hose and started to run warm water into the bottom of the incubators. As the water steamed up and the temperature rose above 100°, then I would open the doors until it dropped to 100° and then close them up again. This went on night and day for two days. Most of the time I spent controlling the incubators in this way and at other times members of the staff would do it. We kept the central heating system stoked up with coke and continued like this for three days. By the fourth day most of the roads were now open, and another turkey producer, who was not hatching at the time, and lived only a few miles away, had some spare capacity in his incubators and his electricity had been restored. So we took all the eggs from our incubators in trays, loaded them on to vans and sent them some 5 miles to the other hatchery, where we left them for a week. After our own electricity supply was restored we brought them back, and they hatched virtually normally, with only a slight reduction on the first hatch.

Although I have had many problems over the years I had been in business, particularly financially, this was the only occasion on which I doubted if I could continue in business.

During 1957 we had a reasonably successful year, although with a fast rate of expansion and the overtrading we were still involved in, we were still short of finance. However, by the end of 1957 I made a point of repaying the bank overdraft of £3,000, and approached the bank again during February 1958 to ask for an overdraft of £8,000. Because of my past problems, particularly so far as lack of financial information was concerned, the bank refused to continue the overdraft. When I asked to have the £3,000 overdraft reinstated I was refused, on the basis that if I needed £8,000, then the bank were not prepared to risk £3,000, because it was not sufficient to carry us through the year.

This information was given to me by the bank manager of Barclays, and I asked at this stage to see the local director who had taken the decision. I had never up to this time met any of the local bank directors.

At my first interview with Mr Gurney of Barclays Bank, his first question to me was why should he lend me money?—and instead of giving what I believe to be the usual answer in such cases, of explaining every detail of why I needed the money, I just made the simple statement: 'Because you will earn 8 per cent on the money you loan to me!'. Although he did not think my answer very constructive, at least he thought it was amusing. He informed me that the bank were not prepared to go on lending me money unless I could justify my financial position through audited figures, and suggested that I change accountants. He introduced me to a man who, as far as I was concerned, had the reputation of acting as a receiver for the bank. I quickly made my position clear to the new accountant that I did not have any intention of allowing my business to go into liquidation, and if that was the plan between the bank and the new accountant, they had better think again.

I informed him that if necessary I would call a meeting of the creditors, because if they tried to close me down during February/March they stood to lose a lot of money, as the majority of the capital at this time of the year was usually invested in new breeding stock. If the breeding stock had to be sold prior to producing turkey chicks during the spring and summer, large amounts of money would be lost, because of the very low value of a breeding hen compared to the income from it if allowed to lay eggs and produce turkey chicks. The difference was something like £1 per bird if sold in the open market, compared with £15 if it were allowed to produce the eggs and chicks.

This point was taken, and gradually there was a return of confidence between myself and the bank through the new financial advisor. It was the first time I had operated under strict financial control, but although I did not like it, I could see the logic of what was happening. There was a complete clamp-down on all capital expenditure, and we allowed the season to continue selling poults as fast as we could go. When the bank accountant had considered my affairs early in March he told me that it was his opinion, and the opinion of the bank, that it would take at least five years to sort out my financial problems. The season went well, we sold poults and day-old turkeys at a good price, and by autumn of that year—only six months after the point when the bank refused any further advances except on the terms of a new financial controller—I had paid back all of the creditors and was actually in credit at the bank; so for the first time during my first eight years in business I did not owe any overdue money, except to the mortgagee on Great Witchingham Hall.

Needless to say, the bank were very pleased that I had been able to achieve this situation, and certainly I was very pleased that their advice to change accountants and bring in tight financial control had paid off in such a handsome way.

Because of the financial success I had enjoyed during 1958, I decided, having cleared all my creditors, that I should go to America during January 1959 to study the American turkey industry. I spent thirty days in the United States, first of all attending the American turkey conference in the mid-west, and following this visiting twenty-eight farms and processing factories. Although the trip was extremely tiring—I had never undertaken such an itinerary before—it was most interesting and gave me the idea of the massive potential within the turkey business.

I telephoned my wife from the States and told her to tell our new financial advisor that he was to go the bank and arrange to borrow as much money as possible. I came back home and made my plans for the building of a business on a much larger scale than I had considered possible before. In the autumn of 1959 I purchased my first aerodrome from the Air Ministry at an auction. This aerodrome covered 360 acres in total, of which 120 were concreted. Very few people could see a use for such a site, and I was able to purchase it for £55 per acre. Today the value of the concrete for breaking alone is worth approximately £400 per acre, and the land value is probably in excess of £300 per acre.

Taking advantage of the runway concrete as floors, I laid out ten large sheds, of 20,000 square feet each, taking two weeks to fill up each shed with turkeys, and starting to place some 10,000 turkeys per week on the aerodrome. I had just got this project going on some scale when I suffered the first outbreak of fowl pest. Fowl pest is a virus disease which is airborne, and therefore cannot be controlled by ordinary disease control methods. Up to this time the Ministry of Agriculture had not allowed the vaccination of any poultry with a fowl pest vaccine, although this was available in many other countries throughout the world. The first flock of birds I had slaughtered were mainly breeding stock, and although the payments were reasonable, they did not fully compensate for the value of the breeding stock on a potential turnover basis. Even so, from the first outbreak of fowl pest I received £50,000 in compensation. This was to be the first of many outbreaks that were to take place over the next three years or so, during which time I was paid approximately one million pounds in compensation by the Government for the slaughter of birds on the various farms which I developed.

The effect of the compensation was the complete disruption of the business in that the breeding stock was slaughtered. I was then paid large sums of money, but had to wait another six months or so before the business became productive again. During this period, although I had received large sums in compensation from the Government, very large numbers of turkeys were slaughtered. In one outbreak alone 193,000 turkeys were slaughtered on one farm during one week.

It is not possible to reconstruct what the financial results profit-wise for the years during which we suffered fowl pest would have been, because of the stock losses which occurred. However, the effect of the fowl pest compensation was that although our trading profits would probably have been as large as those produced by the profits from the Government slaughter policy, we did enjoy one financial advantage from the policy. This arose because all of our breeding stock was valued on a herd basis, in order to keep the value as low as possible; but the effect of this when the birds were slaughtered and compensated for was that the vast majority of money received for this breeding stock was tax free, and we were able during the period 1959–63 to increase the assets of our company by over £400,000. The capital we now received

was used to build and develop the largest turkey business of
its kind in Europe.

Not only did we build the original aerodrome farm, but
we went on to purchase more farms and another aerodrome.
At the same time, we built the first large-scale turkey-
processing factory in the United Kingdom, with a capacity
to kill, pack and freeze over 10,000 turkeys per week. The
rate at which we were investing money, capital expenditure-
wise, can be gauged during this period by the fact that over
the four years 1961–4 the turnover of the company, excluding
compensation, was:

1961	£309,000
1962	£452,000
1963	£771,000
1964	£1,300,000

In addition to the turkeys we were growing on our own
company farms during this period, large numbers of birds
were produced for us by associated farmers, who purchased
the day-old turkeys from us, grew the birds to the required
killing age, and then returned them to us for processing and
marketing. During each year we made the farmer an on-
account payment for the birds we had taken from him, and
at the end of each year we had a profit-sharing scheme and
paid the farmer the balance during the January or February.

At the same time, on the breeding side, we had some twenty
farmers who were producing hatching eggs for us on contract.
This worked quite well, except that it was a very high cost
system; and as the price of turkey meat was reduced during
the large-scale expansion and competitive situation which
developed during this time, we found we could no longer
afford to continue with such a system.

When the Government slaughter policy ceased in 1963
there was automatically a large increase in turkey production
in the UK, because the industry's largest customer had ceased
to purchase! The slaughter policy was replaced by a vaccination policy with a dead vaccine, which proved to be reasonably successful in the early years.

We had little financial information during the fowl pest

I

period which was of much use to us, as we were unable really to run our business on the normal lines at this time, because whenever we built the business back up to size again we would then in the winter of the year suffer a further outbreak of fowl pest. This gave us very little information on which to base any decisions for future policies.

Due to this disruption of our business during 1964 and 1965, with the cessation of the fowl pest slaughter policy we had two years which were not very profitable. We then decided to integrate our business and to devote the whole of our profits to further capital expenditure, in order to achieve the lowest possible costs on production.

From the capital profits which followed from the fowl pest compensation, I started to consider a programme of diversification to get us away from the one-product company situation. This took two forms: first, in conjunction with Dr Napier, our chief geneticist, we planned a rabbit-breeding programme on a large scale. We collected rabbit breeding stock from several different countries in Europe and brought them together, and began a breeding programme on similar lines to that which we had already conducted with turkeys.

Although most people think it is relatively easy to breed rabbits, our experience was that there were far more disease problems than we had had with turkeys. Apart from the disease problems, we found that the price of rabbit meat on the UK market was below the cost of production of the type of organisation which we had set up; and while sales of breeding stock got away to a reasonable start, we found that we could not maintain the programme we had mounted without access to a profitable meat market for reject breeding stock.

The other diversification was into fish farming. Harry Simpson, our present production director, joined us in 1963 in order to develop a commercial fish production programme. We started a pilot scheme, and although we never lost any money producing fish, the problems we came up against were twofold. First, the basic idea of fish production was to use inedible offal from our turkey-processing factory to feed the rainbow trout. In principle this was quite a good idea;

but a few months after we had started the fish pilot project we found that the value of the inedible offal on the meat by-products market had risen to such an extent that it was hardly worthwhile feeding this offal to the fish, because we were getting as much profit from it by selling it in bulk to offal processors. Secondly, following the many months of work which Mr Simpson carried out in Norfolk surveying streams and potential sites for a fish farm, we discovered that a great deal of the Norfolk water was polluted to varying degrees; and where really good sites were found, it was impossible to purchase them as the owners were not prepared to sell.

However, we did succeed in carrying out a certain amount of research work on the production of rainbow trout, and our production at one stage did reach something like half a ton of fish during one year.

In addition to these two diversifications into other animal products, we also decided to begin a hatchery in North Italy, as we found that there was a tremendous demand for day-old turkeys in Italy, where the breast meat of turkey was being used as a substitute for veal, which is consumed on a very large scale by the Northern Italian population.

Having set up our hatchery in Italy, we had no problems in selling the output. The only problem we came up against with the Italians was that having sold the day-old turkeys, we had great difficulty in collecting the cash! We finally had to write off something like £20,000 of bad debts within this enterprise.

In 1966 we realised that we were going to require all of the cash generated from our basic turkey business to expand and streamline this part of our business activity, so we took a decision to close down all of our diversification projects and to concentrate solely upon the turkey business.

From 1967 onwards we started to buy new sites and construct sheds on the new sites and the existing sites in order to replace the turkeys which, up to this point, had been grown for us on contract by local farmers. The rate at which this programme was being developed can be seen from the fact that the breeding on our own farms in 1966 was approximately 700,000 birds per annum, while by 1967 this had been more than doubled to 1,500,000 birds per annum.

Not only had we taken up the production of the vast majority of turkeys produced outside for us on contract, but we had also expanded our total sales by something approaching 50 per cent. The result of this decision, coupled with a rather better market price, had a dramatic effect upon our profitability. From a profit of £40,000 in 1966, our profits for 1967 advanced to £253,000. Coupled with depreciation of over £80,000 per annum and no dividends being paid, we were now generating a cash flow of over £200,000 per annum.

At the same time that our integration and expansion was taking place, we were conducting experimental research on a large scale to try and find the best environment for the turkeys, in order to obtain the lowest production costs. This programme was carried out by another of our staff geneticists, Dr McFarquhar, and we found that by controlling the amount of light given to the birds, ventilation rates, and temperature, we were able to make a significant reduction in cost.

At the same time we changed over to completely automatic feeding systems, and began a research programme on the nutritional requirements of our strains of birds. Again our success with this research was even better than anybody in the company could have forecast, for we found that with our particular strains of birds, they would respond very well to a comparatively low plane of nutrition. In addition we carried out further experiments on the amount of square footage that each bird required to grow and achieve its optimum performance; and we found that we were able to make considerable changes to our stocking rates, and increase the number of birds in each of our sheds very significantly. This last factor we found was only possible in a situation where we could control light within the sheds, and therefore the total environment.

We were fortunate to have carried out this experimental work and to have taken the decision to integrate, for following the reasonable market price of 1967, the price per lb. of turkey started to decline again in 1968 in the market place, and we were able, through our significant cost reductions and expanding volume, to produce and maintain profits on a similar level to those of 1967.

During 1968, 1969 and 1970 we saw continuing low prices for turkeys within the UK, and although through our increased efficiency we had been able to maintain our profitability, many of our medium-sized competitors were forced to leave the field because they were unprofitable.

During this period we were able to increase our share of the turkey market quite considerably, and found, on examining the accounts of those of our competitors who were still in business, that whilst we had made an average of something like a 20 per cent return on total capital employed during the 1968/69/70 period, many competitors were either unprofitable or were producing profits at very low levels. This could mean only one thing—that our cost of production was considerably below theirs.

This gave us the confidence to continue our expansion policy. During the years from 1966 to 1970 our turnover was nearly doubled, whilst our profits had increased eight times.

For the past three years, apart from the production of whole oven-ready birds, we have been continuing considerable development work on other uses for turkey meat, because we know that basically the turkey is a highly efficient producer of lean meat and has few competitors cost-wise as a lean meat producer among other farm animals. This development work has taken several different aspects.

First, we have looked at the fresh meat market, and we are now supplying some 50,000-plus birds per annum into this market, where the birds are cut up completely, the breast meat sold in slices, the giblets, thigh meat and drumsticks sold as separate products.

It is now the view within our company that this is one of the great potentials for us in the future, particularly as we enter the EEC, where we shall see an even wider differential between the price of red meat and turkey meat. Because of its large size, the turkey has a distinct advantage over the chicken in providing meat for cutting up, in that the labour cost per lb. of meat produced is significantly lower with turkey than it would be with chicken. In addition, at the moment the consumption of turkey in the UK is only approximately 2 lb. per capita, whilst that of chicken is over 20 lb. per capita. We therefore feel there is an opportunity for us to supply an alternative form of meat to the British housewife in order to give more variation to the total diet at comparatively low cost.

THE COMPANY IN 1971

The company went public towards the end of 1971 and it may perhaps be useful to describe it as it was when the shares were offered to the public. We employed approximately 460 people. By this time we had a profit-sharing scheme for our executives, based on the return on capital employed. In 1963 we had established an optional contributory pension fund and life assurance scheme which was available to all our monthly paid staff.

By 1971 our original premises of Great Witchingham Hall had ceased to be occupied by turkeys. We had moved them into other accommodation and converted the hall into offices. The turkeys were moved into specially designed turkey houses made of timber and asbestos. We had eighty-nine of them, occupying a total floor area of nearly 2 million square feet. Over the years the company had acquired a number of sites in the vicinity of Great Witchingham Hall and by 1971 the total area was close on 1,000 acres.

A processing plant had been built in the grounds of Great Witchingham Hall with an annual capacity for processing $2\frac{1}{2}$ million oven-ready turkeys and a cold store with a capacity to hold 200,000 turkeys.

From 1959 we employed geneticists to work on the scientific breeding of turkeys. Our most successful strain is known as the Matthews Ten-30 strain. It combines exceptional reproductive performance with good meat production. In addition to the breeding research programme, the company had built up a team of some twenty-five people involved in environmental and nutritional research, which covers in particular the design and management of turkey rearing houses and formulation of turkey feeds in respect of both the breeding and commercial growing flocks. The company rented an IBM computer which is installed at Great Witchingham Hall and on which all research data was both recorded and analysed.

A health laboratory was also maintained, controlled by a professional bacteriologist assisted by qualified staff. This laboratory undertook the constant surveillance of the health status of both the growing and the breeding birds and examined the effectiveness of all cleaning and hygiene procedures.

The hatchery had a capacity to incubate 110,000 eggs per week. It had its own water-conditioning plant, central heating system, and stand-by generating plant so that a failure of the electricity supply could not jeopardise the incubation process. The company had developed and built turkey-rearing houses in which light, ventilation and temperature could be closely controlled at optimum levels for stock comfort and efficient production. After the initial brooding stage, watering and feeding was automatic.

The turkey-rearing houses were situated on five separate sites, all of which are within 25 miles of Great Witchingham Hall. The growing of turkeys in a controlled environment had led to a significant reduction in production costs. As far as possible each of the company's rearing sites subdivided into small groups of houses operated on an all-in, all-out basis so that the presence at the same time of both young and old birds on a site was kept to a minimum. By 1971 the company was the largest integrated turkey producer in Europe. Production exceeded 2 million birds per annum.

Every aspect of the integrated production of turkeys was undertaken by the company, from the breeding of pedigree birds through to the processing and freezing in oven-ready form. Throughout the 1960s approximately 90 per cent of the company's sales were in the form of frozen oven-ready turkeys. The balance of the company's sales were in fresh turkeys, both whole and in cut portions, and also in breeding stock and hatching eggs for commercial growing stock.

Over this period the annual availability of turkeys in

frozen and fresh form in the United Kingdom increased from approximately 5½ million birds in 1962 to 13 million in 1970. This represents an overall rate of expansion of the order of 11 per cent per annum. By 1970 the company estimated that its sales represented approximately 17 per cent of the total turkey market and 22 per cent in frozen oven-ready form.

The growth of the market for turkeys can largely be attributed to two factors: first, the overall reduction in price as compared with continuous increases in the price of red meats; and second, the development of sales at times other than Christmas, in particular at Easter and other holiday periods. For example, by 1970 consumption of turkeys at Christmas is believed to represent about 50 per cent of total annual consumption, whereas in earlier years this amounted to as much as 80 per cent. In addition, there was a considerable increase in sales throughout the year and the sale of turkey in cut portions expanded. We were the first producer of the 'mini' turkey, which weighs between 5 and 7 lb., and this played an important part in the expansion of the company's sales.

The company sold to approximately one hundred customers, sales being almost equally divided between the wholesale and retail trades. Among the famous high street outlets served by the company are Baxters (Butchers), the Co-op, Dewhurst, Fine Fare, Mac Fisheries and J. Sainsbury. The company also served major meat and poultry whole-

Table 6.1 Growth of Turnover and Profit, 1965–71

Year:	Turnover	Net profit before tax
	£	£
1965	2,023,000	5,500
1966	2,006,000	41,000
1967	2,234,000	254,000
1968	2,675,000	231,000
1969	3,162,000	266,000
1970	3,509,000	324,000
1971	4,453,000	877,000

salers, and a range of frozen food wholesalers and mail order houses including Littlewoods. The company's sales policy has been to contract on a forward basis for the major part of its output, and sales have generally been made two to four months ahead of production.

The growth of the company's profits over the period 1965–71 are in shown in Table 6.1.

GOING PUBLIC

Having built the business up to profits of approximately £250,000 per annum, I found that there were considerable problems on my personal front as far as finance was concerned. First of all, the whole of the wealth that I had created was tied up within Bernard Matthews Ltd and I had no assets outside the company at all. The company owned the house I lived in, most of the furniture, my car, and virtually every other asset. In addition, I had the further disadvantage that I had a private overdraft at the bank of some considerable scale. This had come about for two reasons: one was that in putting 18 per cent of the equity of Bernard Matthews in trust for my children I had to pay capital gains tax on this, and had to borrow at the bank to cover this situation. In addition, my wife and I had made certain insurance arrangements over the years to cover each other in the event of death and the subsequent estate duty liabilities. This meant that we were paying thousands of pounds per annum in insurance premiums to cover hundreds of thousands of pounds worth of potential liability for estate duty purposes.

Although on the business side I was already a wealthy man, when one considered the potential value or even the asset value of the company, on my private side I was distinctly hard up!

In early 1970 my professional advisors and I agreed that we should start to take steps to seek a public flotation to realise some of the profit which we had accumulated within the company.

We discussed the matter with Kleinwort Benson in the

autumn of 1969. This was during a period of extreme bank credit control, and in addition to discussing our possible flotation with them, we also secured their agreement to a £250,000 acceptance credit. I should make it clear that at this stage our problem was not that we were un-credit-worthy: the bank would have been only too pleased to lend us more money to expand, for by this time we had established a successful record with strong accounting control. The problem was that they were not allowed to do so under the Bank of England regulations then in force. Kleinwort Benson agreed to loan us the £250,000 and to work with us towards flotation. An accountant's report was prepared. This was comparatively simple in our case, because Kleinwort Benson accepted that Dixon, Wilson, Tubbs and Gillett, our auditors, who had been auditors to the company for the past two or three years, were also acceptable to them as reporting accountants.

After some six months, Kleinwort Benson made a proposal to us which my professional advisors and I found unattractive. Their first proposal was that we should sell 48 per cent of the equity in the company to the public and two-thirds of the resulting availability of cash should be used to refund bank overdrafts, leaving only a relatively small amount of money for my family and myself. I decided that as a matter of policy we should improve our liquidity and await flotation for another year or so.

Some two to three months later, after I had arrived at this decision, I was unfortunate enough to sustain a coronary thrombosis, and this in any event obviously excluded any chance of an immediate flotation. On medical advice I was ordered to cease work within the company for a period of up to six months, which I did, and I am pleased to say that my heart damage is now completely repaired.

During the six months period that I was away, at least one advantage appeared, and that was that, although I had been the chairman and managing director of the company since its inception, during my absence my co-directors proved themselves able to manage the company very successfully, for during this period they produced the largest profit that we had ever produced since the day I started the business. Quite embarrassing!

I returned to the business in April 1971 and again began to look at the question of flotation.

Kleinwort Benson put a further proposal to us, giving us some idea of their valuation of the company, which I should state did not accord with mine! After many discussions, and in some cases strong arguments, concerning the valuation—which almost brought us to a change of merchant bankers!—I finally decided, having seen the strength of their arguments, that their idea of the PE ratio of the company was probably more correct than mine.

We came to the stock market on 16 November 1971, with a forecast profit of £700,000, and a total price tag on the company of £4 million. Of the 4 million 25p shares issued we offered 1,600,000 to the public at 100p per share; 600,000 of the shares offered being sold by my trustees, 500,000 by myself and 500,000 by my wife.

The net inflow of funds to my family was in the order of £1,500,000, and my family still controlled nearly 60 per cent of the company after flotation. Although we were over-subscribed, our share performance in the early days after flotation confirmed that Kleinwort Benson's views were right and mine were wrong; for although we offered the shares at 100p, and many other issues during this period got off to a good start, in our own case we opened at a discount, with the shares dropping to as low as 93p during the first few weeks.

We beat our £700,000 profit forecast, which we knew was a very conservative figure, very handsomely, producing profits of £877,000; and our share price moved within six months from its opening discounted position of 93p to a price of over 150p.

7 Fidelity Radio

Fidelity Radio was set up by Jack Dickman in 1946 with a capital of £350 and an initial output of six radio sets. Twenty-five years later the company was the largest manufacturer of radios in the United Kingdom. The story begins in the East End of London, where Jack Dickman was born in 1916. His father was a fur skin merchant living in Bethnal Green. Mr Dickman senior had been born in Russia and emigrated to Britain sometime before the First World War. There was not much money in the skin trade in the period between the two world wars and the family did not have much to spare. They lived in a council flat and Jack Dickman was sent to the local council school.

At the age of ten Jack Dickman won a scholarship to the Central Foundation School. He passed the old Matric. examination and left when he was sixteen. His first job was working as a fur cutter in a workshop. It was natural for him to go into this line because of his father's business interests in skins.

Towards the end of the 1930s the menace of Hitler grew greater every year. In 1938 Jack Dickman joined the Territorials and when war was declared in 1939 he was immediately called up into the army. In 1942 he was posted to work on radar and it was during the later years of the war, while he was engaged on this work, that he acquired most of his knowledge of radio and electronics. It was this experience that was to determine the course of his career for the next twenty-five years.

FOUNDATION OF THE COMPANY, 1946

On being demobilised from the army in 1946 Jack Dickman had to find some means of earning a living. He had married during the war and had a small son, and the prospects in the fur business did not seem particularly good. So he decided that he would try to put the knowledge of radios acquired in the army to good use and set up in business as a manufacturer of radio sets. At that time the standard radios were Utility models and they were hardly glamorous products. Jack Dickman thought he could design and make something a bit more attractive.

In setting up the business and getting started there were a number of problems. First it was necessary to find premises, and a small place was found in Silchester Road, London, W.10. The rent was 15s per week. Second, a good deal of bureaucracy had to be fought. At first Jack Dickman imagined that all he had to do was to procure the necessary parts and get to work. But he had reckoned without the requirements of bureaucracy. He found that he needed a manufacturer's licence before he could even begin to operate. It was necessary to have steel and timber allocations as well. So he made the proper overtures to the sponsoring Ministry and to his dismay was flatly refused permission to manufacture. The ruling was that only pre-war and wartime manufacturers were to be granted permits to continue in business in the immediate post-war period.

Jack Dickman is not a man to take no for an answer too readily and he badgered everyone he could approach at the Ministry. He pleaded that there was a vast market waiting for something more stylish and modern than the Utility radios. He even played on the fact that he was an exserviceman trying to make his way in the brave new world. Eventually he won and was granted a licence to make not more than fifty sets a quarter.

Another problem was money. Jack Dickman started with about £350. Some of it came from his own savings and the gratuity which he received on being demobbed from the army, some of it came from Mr S. Dickman and the rest came as a loan from Mrs Dickman's mother. The family were pretty short of money in those early days but they managed.

The enterprise was now ready to begin work. The first

production was a batch of six radios. Jack Dickman piled them into a taxi, took them around West End dealers and was welcomed with open arms. No one could say the radios looked Utility although they look rather dated today. Demand was good and Jack Dickman found he could sell all he could make. This first Fidelity radio was a five-valve, two-band set and sold at 17 guineas; twenty years later the company was producing a vastly more sophisticated three-band transistor set at almost half the price.

After nine months of hard work the demand for the Fidelity sets was so great that it became necessary to look for larger premises. The company was by now employing four men to assemble the sets. Eventually a disused public house was found in Blechynden Street, only 500 yards from Silchester Road, and here the company started to make radiograms in batches of twelve at a time.

In a short space of time, demand again outgrew the available facilities, and four railway arches across the road were acquired as additional production space. The result was a significant increase in the production of radiograms and radios and the company also began to produce record players.

By 1962 the company's operations were scattered around several locations in West London in some 24,000 square feet of factory and office floor space. Blechynden Street by now had been taken over by the administration and the service department. Once more the problem arose of finding more floor space, and more particularly of concentrating the facilities under one roof if possible.

Jack Dickman was anxious not to have to move out of West London largely because he did not want to break up the labour force that had been built up over the years. Eventually, suitable premises were found at 6 Olaf Street. It was a vacant building of 65,000 square feet, previously used by the LCC as a supplies depot for the Fire Service. By the end of 1964 the company had closed all its former scattered premises and everything was concentrated in Olaf Street.

Since its early beginnings Fidelity Radio has manufactured four main types of products, namely radios, record players, tape recorders and audios, and the development of each of these products will now be described in turn.

RADIOS

As already described, the first products were radios. The models were technically conventional but were distinctive in design and their success was due to a combination of this distinctiveness of design and the low price.

The company did not enter the field of technically advanced radios until the late 1950s. In 1958 the company produced its first transistor radio, which was called the Ayr, and some months later a second model called the Florida. Both of these were quite large models and sold well.

In 1960 the company produced the first miniature transistor radio in Britain. It measured $4'' \times 2\frac{1}{4}'' \times 1\frac{1}{4}''$ and was called the Coronet. The advance in this model was that the casing was moulded in plastic and it was through this technique that it was possible to produce such a small model. The chief competitors were the Japanese, but Fidelity was helped in its competition against them by the tariff barriers and also by the quotas on Japanese imports.

The company produced a number of different models during the 1960s. Towards the end of the decade the models were called the Rad 11, the Rad 11B and the Rad 12. They are all small transistor sets. Over the years 1968–71 Rad 12 has sold about 110,000 sets each year. In the early 1970s the company had eight models in current production. By this time Fidelity had 41 per cent of the British radio market and was the largest manufacturer of radios in Great Britain. Jack Dickman thinks that the company's success in obtaining this large share of the British market has been due partly to their feeling for the style of design which would appeal to the British public. This is because the management team is so closely in touch with the British people, and it is here that the company has an advantage over its competitors in Japan and Hong Kong.

RADIOGRAMS AND RECORD PLAYERS

It was in 1948 that Fidelity produced its first record player. It was called the 11FI and it sold around 24,000 models. The success of the company's models has been due principally to their low price. The first record player sold at £18 as compared with around £28 to £30 for most of the other models on the market. There was nothing particularly outstanding technically about most of Fidelity's record players. Their success was due principally to their low price.

An exception to this policy of selling on price occurred in 1971 when the company pioneered a new technical process. This was the structural foam plastic record player. Structural foam is a special kind of plastic which can be moulded in a thicker structure than is possible with conventional plastic. It can be moulded up to half an inch thick. This gives it an appearance of solidity. It is also acoustically as good as wood in so far as it does not vibrate with loud bass notes.

The development of this structural foam record player took place in the following way. In 1969 Jack Dickman read an account of the development of structural foam in a trade journal. He realised the potential of the process for moulding the casing of record players and so the company set to work to mould a player in the new structural foam. A prototype was produced and was put into production in 1971. In this year the company was the market leader in record players in Britain and had 29 per cent of the British market.

TAPE RECORDS

Fidelity first began the manufacture of tape recorders in 1958. The first models were the Argyle and the Argyle Minor. There were problems in manufacturing them because they were made in wood cabinets, and it was impossible to find suppliers of these cabinets who could deliver them in sufficient quantities and on time.

Because of this difficulty Jack Dickman began to think of plastic as a possible material. He searched for a suitable technique and hit on the one known as 'deposition tooling'. This is a moulding process in which a plastic cabinet can be moulded in a single unit. The company designed the tools, mouldings and machines and produced the first plastic tape recorder cabinet in 1960. It was called the Playmaster, and it has been the best selling British manufactured tape recorder. In the early 1960s some 5,000 of these models were sold per week.

Between 1963 and 1968 Fidelity produced another model named the Studio, which was generally more sophisticated, and in 1966 it produced the Playmaster Major. Throughout the 1960s Fidelity was selling something of the order of 70,000 tape recorders per year. But this market collapsed badly in 1968 when purchase tax of $33\frac{1}{3}$ per cent was imposed on tape recorders. At about the same time the cassette began to be marketed and this further reduced the market for conventional tape recorders. As a result, the company's annual sales dropped from about 70,000 per year to about 30,000. Fortunately this did not damage the firm greatly because its transistors and record players were doing well.

AUDIOS

The company's fourth and final major product is the audio. The audio is a development of the radiogram. It houses two speakers in separate cabinets which should ideally be placed about 10 feet from each other, and is used for stereophonic records.

Fidelity entered the audio market in 1970. Usually the company has produced at the lower price end of the market, as has been noted, but this time a different policy was adopted and the company made a high priced machine. On this occasion Jack Dickman felt that if it proved possible to sell a high priced model the company should be able to do better still with a cheaper model.

In 1971 Fidelity went into production and manufactured the Unit Audio 1. This model was given the Design Centre Award for the excellence of its design, and was also recommended by *Which?* as the best buy in audios. By the end of

K

1971 Fidelity was one of the leading brands in audios in Britain and had about 20 per cent of the market.

PROFITABILITY OF THE COMPANY

Naturally in its early days Fidelity did not make a great deal of money and in fact the Dickman family had to economise carefully so that a substantial proportion of the profits could be ploughed back into the business to finance expansion. But the profits increased steadily from the first establishment of the company, until by the end of the 1950s they were up to around £50,000 per year. The turnover and profits from 1962 to 1971 are set out in Table 7.1.

Table 7.1   Growth of Turnover and Profits, 1962–71

Year ended March 31st:	Turnover £	Profits before directors' emoluments and before taxation £
1962	1,549,431	69,354
1963	1,869,940	117,492
1964	2,092,688	75,812
1965	2,027,515	50,858
1966	1,799,807	46,927
1967	1,957,854	52,744
1968	2,238,594	119,179
1969	2,590,650	169,975
1970	2,671,454	140,795
1971	4,070,725	347,458

FINANCING THE COMPANY

As stated earlier, when Jack Dickman began in 1946 he had accumulated £350 from various sources. Over the period 1946–51 he tried to borrow from banks but none of them would give overdraft facilities. There were considerable financial worries. Jack had to devise various ways of financing. One policy was to sell to customers who paid quickly and another to pay the company's own debts to its suppliers as late as possible.

In 1952 a bank allowed the company a small overdraft to carry it over wages day. But Fidelity received no help of any significance from any bank until the early 1960s, when overdraft facilities for about £20,000 were secured. It is ironic that today the banks would bend over backwards to lend anything up to a million pounds but Fidelity no longer needs the money.

In 1971 the company went public. There were 4 million shares in total, and those offered to the public were priced at 70p, thus indicating that the company was worth something of the order of £2,800,000. The shares were heavily oversubscribed, and within two months of flotation the price of the shares on the stock market had risen to 125p, giving the company a value of £5 million.

INCENTIVES AND COMPANY MORALE

Jack Dickman believes firmly in paying a good deal of attention to keeping all members of the company contented and happy, so that they will give their best to the company. From time to time he has given shares in the company to some of the directors, partly as a reward for their services and partly to give them a stake in the future growth of the company. In 1960 $2\frac{1}{2}$ per cent of the shares were given to the sales director. In 1967 $2\frac{1}{2}$ per cent of shares were given to the company secretary and financial director. Jack Dickman's eldest son joined the company as works director and he also has a $2\frac{1}{2}$ per cent shareholding for his work in this capacity.

As works director, Jack Dickman's eldest son looks after the general question of the morale of the labour force. Father and son discuss the problems together frequently in the evenings. Fidelity now have 370 employees, all working at the premises in London. The company has a variety of ways of helping and caring for its personnel. It gives them interest-free loans up to several hundred pounds for such purposes as buying houses, furniture and so forth. Fidelity workers earn much higher wages than average. The basic rates are higher than the trade union rates, and the company also pays a substantial production bonus. This is a collective bonus which is paid each week and varies with the previous week's productivity. These bonus payments can be of the order of £12 to £14 per week and are of course considerable. In return, Fidelity expects its staff to give more than average effort. The company's relationship with the labour force is very good and there has never been any industrial unrest.

Jack Dickman knows all the foremen in the business personally and also many of the assembly personnel. He knows something about their personal circumstances and they often talk informally when Jack Dickman walks through the factory.

Fidelity does not give exceptional holidays. The company gives two weeks on full pay to new employees and three weeks on full pay to employees who have been with the company for more than two years. But the company is fairly generous about sickness. It supplements the national health payments to bring the total payments up to the normal level.

PERSONAL MOTIVATIONS

It is never easy to know the nature of one's motivation but Jack Dickman has some views on what has motivated his work in building up Fidelity Radio over a period of a quarter of a century or so. In the first place, the chief motive was certainly not to make a lot of money. The motive has been more in the nature of a creative impulse. He has enjoyed the challenge of producing the best product for a particular price and of a particular quality for the mass market. He would not be particularly interested in making an expensive new one-off product for some specific purpose. Nor would he have liked to have worked in a service industry. He does not feel that this would have satisfied the creative impulse which has been an important part of his motivation.

I asked Jack Dickman whether he has found that the life of an entrepreneur demands a lot of hard work. He replied that possibly it did. In the early days he used to work about sixteen hours a day, seven days a week, but he has been able to let up a bit in more recent years. Nevertheless, the life of an entrepreneur is never a nine-to-five routine.

8　Lotus Cars

Colin Chapman was born in 1928 in the London suburb of Hornsey. His father was the landlord of the Railway Hotel, and it was there that he grew up. Like many boys, the young Colin Chapman was interested in cars. After leaving school he went to London University to study engineering and it was during his time as a student that Colin Chapman built his first racing car.

This was in the years immediately following the end of the Second World War. At that time the normal principle in building racing cars was to build the biggest possible engine into the traditional, steel-bodied, aluminium-tanked car with a multi-tubular chassis. This presented Colin Chapman with a difficulty because he was not able to afford a big engine. Necessity proved the mother of invention, and he was forced to take a different approach. The one he adopted was to lighten the body work while at the same time keeping the car safe through improvements in aerodynamic design. This aim—the improvement of power/weight ratios—has been one of the most important principles in the development of Lotus cars.

1948: THE FIRST LOTUS

Colin Chapman built his first racing car in 1948. He bought an Austin Seven, improved the engine and built a light body for it in bonded plywood. It was driven in two events and had a class win in each. But the pressure of university work was severe and for a time Colin Chapman put his hobby aside to cope with the impending examinations.

The next year, 1949, afforded more leisure and Colin Chapman made another racing car. This time he again used an Austin Seven chassis, but the engine used was a Ford Ten.

Again he used the same strategy of attempting to lighten the bodywork beyond the limits generally considered safe at the time. This was a highly original approach. The great majority of people take what has already been established and try to improve on it or make small changes, and it is an unusual man who can go back to first principles, assess what the basic reason is for doing anything and find the most straightforward and simple way of doing it. It is this quality of creativity that Colin Chapman possesses and it has been one of the most important factors underlying his success.

In his early days, Colin Chapman became dissatisfied with trying to unite structures that contained multi-tubular chassis and aluminium fuel tanks, and drivers, and bodywork—elements which never seemed to fit together nicely. You'd build the steel structure to carry the loads. And then you'd cover the whole thing with a fibre-glass body. This struck Colin Chapman as three elements which could be replaced by one. If you designed the aluminium tank in the first place such that it would hold a front and rear suspension, then you could do away with the steel frame. And if you could also design the aluminium fuel tank in the first place such that it conformed to the required body shape, then you could do away with the body. So in one operation you reduced a three-element structure to a one-element structure—with a consequent gain all round in terms of lightness, stiffness and cost. And this provides an ideal solution. Colin Chapman remembers sketching this theory on the back of a napkin at a lunch table, after talking about cars with someone. But this was probably only the result of subconsciously worrying about it for six months. Chapman believes that all good engineers have to be a bit of an artist. In other words, they've got to appreciate simplicity and elegance. In all sorts of design, you can suddenly think of something so simple that you can't understand why you didn't think of it before.

After graduating from the university Colin Chapman went into the RAF, and when he came out he took a job with British Aluminium. During his spare time he continued to build racing cars. The building was done in a lock-up garage in Muswell Hill, North London. Within a couple of years there was quite a demand for replicas of the Lotus cars and he therefore decided to set up a company to produce them.

1952: THE FORMATION OF THE LOTUS ENGINEERING COMPANY

It was in 1952 that the company was formed. Colin Chapman had very little capital and in fact he borrowed £25 from his fiancée to help keep the company in funds. The company's product was a set of components which enabled purchasers to build their own Lotus cars. The factory was a small lean-to in Hornsey. Three full-time employees were taken on. Normally Colin Chapman would put on his overalls and start work as soon as he got home in the evening and put in fairly long hours. His fiancée did the company's paper work.

Up to this point all the cars had been based on Austin chassis and (except for the first) on Ford engines. But the sixth car was designed on new principles. It had a multi-tube spaceframe, which was clad with light alloy panels. It weighed only 90 lb. without the engine and was a considerable success. Well over a hundred were eventually produced. Variously, using Ford Ten, Ford Consul, BMW and MG engines, they were raced throughout the world—from Canada in the west to Australia in the east.

But there were financial problems. In the latter half of 1952, Lotus Engineering ran into financial difficulties. The three employees had to be laid off and Chapman kept the business going on his own, with the help of his fiancée who dealt with the growing mountain of paper. He spent the next year or so building his first Lotus 6 chassis on his own.

By the following year—1953—these financial problems were under control and the demand for the car was booming. The prospects of the business seemed sufficiently promising for Chapman to give up his job in British Aluminium and work for Lotus full time. About the same time he formed a team of drivers to race the cars and this was called Team Lotus.

The company continued to operate for another five years at Hornsey, until 1958. Over this period several innovations were made. In 1956, the first Lotus Formula 2 car was exhibited at the London Motor Show. It was powered by a 1500 cc Coventry Climax engine, and afterwards performed very satisfactorily in the hands of Innes Ireland. In 1957 came the first of the Elites (of which 988 were eventually manufactured), powered by a 1216 cc Coventry Climax engine which had a top speed of 130 mph. And then, in the following year, the first Formula 1 Lotus was built.

1958: THE MOVE TO CHESHUNT AND THE FIRST REAR-ENGINED LOTUS

By 1958 the premises at Hornsey were too small to handle the demand for the cars and it became necessary to look around for larger premises. A factory was found further out of London, at Cheshunt, and the company moved there during the course of 1958.

In the following year Colin Chapman made a radical change in the overall construction of the cars by designing a rear-engined model. In those days, only Cooper in F1 and Porsche in F2 had got around to putting the engines at the rear. Lotus, in company with all the others, mounted it at the front. For some time Chapman had been worrying about the basic principle of where was the right place for an engine in a racing car, and eventually he decided that it was somewhere between the driver and the back axle. A model was designed on this principle and it was ready for racing for the 1960 season. Innes Ireland soon showed that it had all the characteristics necessary to win races, and Stirling Moss carried the proof a stage further when he gave Lotus its first Grand Prix victory by winning the Monaco Grand Prix of that year.

It was particularly at this time that Colin Chapman considers he learned that all the best endeavours, in the fields of both engineering and business, are accomplished by very close-knit teamwork, with each member of the team contributing his own particular skill. He regards his own function as that of the coordinator of the team, providing general policy guidance.

LOTUS DRIVERS

For success in car racing it is essential to have the best drivers as well as to design good cars. This was one of the places where good team work was necessary. One of the company's most important steps was the recruitment of Jim Clark in 1959. At the time Jim Clark was under contract to Reg Parnell, with the object of driving a Grand Prix Aston Martin which never quite made it. On one occasion he was testing at Goodwood when Mike Costin turned up with a Formula Junior Lotus. He asked Clark whether he would like to give the car a run and afterwards comment on it.

Clark's impression, as recorded in his book *Jim Clark at the Wheel*, was as follows: 'After testing the Grand Prix Aston, I leapt into the Lotus Junior and, oh, my goodness, the Lotus in comparison was simply fantastic. I wouldn't have believed that any car could hold the road the way this Lotus did. I could go through St Mary's, the off-camber left hander with the deep dip in the middle, so quickly that I didn't think it was possible. The car seemed to be glued to the road.'

After this favourable impression Jim Clark seemed destined to join the Lotus company, but the way that Jim Clark actually did so was rather odd. Colin Chapman was intending to use John Surtees, whom he had given a contract. But at the time of both the Dutch and Belgian Grands Prix of 1960, Surtees had motor cycling commitments and couldn't turn up. Suddenly Team Lotus was short of drivers. It was obvious that the Aston Martin project wasn't going to amount to anything, so Chapman approached Clark, who thankfully accepted. In the Dutch event, which was Clark's first Formula 1 drive, the gearbox developed a fault when he was lying in fourth place. In the Belgian race, he finished fifth. It was not until the Pau Grand Prix of the following year that Clark, who had now become a member of Team Lotus, had his first F1 victory.

Taken together the abilities of Colin Chapman and Jim Clark made a powerful race-winning combination. Although

Jim won the World Championship only twice, he beat Fangio's record of twenty-four Grand Prix victories, and did it in less time than it took the Argentinian ace driver. But there must also be another record here, for Clark was always loyal to Lotus. From that early drive at Zandvoort, he never competed in another make of Formula 1 car. Fangio drove for Alfa Romeo, Ferrari, Maserati and Mercedes. Jim Clark drove only for Lotus.

For the 1962 season Chapman designed yet another model. Its frame was virtually stripped to two petrol tanks and it earned the first World Construction Prize. In all Jim Clark won thirty-two major international races in Lotus cars. It was a great tragedy for the company when he died in a crash during a race in Germany in April 1968.

1965: THE MOVE TO HETHEL

During the early 1960s the company grew steadily. The Elite was selling well; Team Lotus was busy in F1, F2 and Formula Junior, and an Indianapolis car was on the drawing board for the 1963 event. Two years after this, the factory had to be moved again. The premises at Cheshunt, which had seemed so spacious after the Hornsey set-up, appeared suddenly to have shrunk.

A number of locations were considered. Eventually a World War II airfield was found at Hethel, near Norwich. Hethel is such a small village that you could drive through it without noticing it's there. The airfield is bounded on one side by a cluster of black hangars, and on the others by sky. It is a bleak and bare landscape—typically East Anglian, with absolutely no suggestion of the closed-in clutter of buildings that town-dwellers prefer. It was chosen primarily because of the availability of labour, and also because there was a landing strip for the company's aircraft and room for a test track. The latter is a matter of considerable pride to Lotus people. Even Jaguar has not had one of its own.

In addition to the necessity of finding first-class drivers the company has had to obtain first-class engine designers. In the late 1960s Lotus had used the engine designed by

Keith Duckworth and Mike Costin. Their firm is called Cosworth Engineering. Keith Duckworth worked with the company for a summer vacation while he was an engineering student, and Lotus has generally used his engines in the Formula 1 cars.

It was with a Cosworth engine that Graham Hill won the World Championship in 1968, and Lotus won the constructors' award. But engines alone do not win races, and it is a difficult truth about cars that having more power to play with adds to a designer's stock of problems. For one thing, the power has to be transmitted to the road wheels; for another, the resulting product must have extremely good road-holding characteristics.

If Lotus was beset by a particular problem during the late 1960s, it has been in the area of transmission. The company had a spate of difficulties in the drive line of its Formula 1 cars and this was due almost entirely to inability to obtain the necessary parts from sub-contractors in the British motor industry in time to match the advance in design the company had made in wheel grip.

Road-holding is easier. Having discovered the answer, Lotus can apply it themselves. There are no sub-contractors involved. The latest solution can reasonably be summed up as the 'wedge-shaped principle'. It is applied to the Formula 1 car, to the Lotus 47 sports car, and—though, perhaps, to a lesser extent—to the Elans. It arose primarily from aerodynamic studies from which Colin Chapman suddenly realised that, with the extremely high power-to-weight ratio of modern racing cars, the concept of minimising drag should become secondary to that of minimising lift.

THE SPORTS CAR

By the end of the 1960s the company was producing four different sports car models, designed to meet a wide range of the market. These were the Lotus +2 S130, which sold in 1970 at a recommended price of £2,710. The Elan Sprint sold at £1,720, the Lotus Europa at £1,478 and the Lotus 7 S4 at £995.

The Lotus +2 S130 and the Elan have the same engine, which the company manufactures itself. It is a 1558 cc twin cam engine that was first produced in 1963. During the 1960s the company produced some 20,000 of these engines, a large proportion being sold to the Ford Motor Company for fitment in the Cortina Lotus and Ford Escort Twin Cam models. The company manufactures the bulk of its components including the fibre-glass bodies.

The company's four models differ partly in the comfort they afford. At the lower end of the market, the 7 S4 is in the somewhat spartan sports car tradition. The first models were of this vintage sports car type. Later models of the car were built with greater emphasis on comfort.

The company introduced the Elan in 1962, and the Lotus Europa and the Lotus +2 in 1967. The more expensive and later models have been more in the tradition of the grand tourer. The growth of production of the cars is shown in Table 8.1.

1968 : GOING PUBLIC

Lotus went public in October 1968. The company offered 862,000 ordinary shares at a nominal price of 2s and an asking price of £1 10s and were modestly oversubscribed. The PE ratio was 23·8 and was the highest ever for a non-tender offer sale. This means of course that the price put on the shares was high, since it valued the company at well over thirteen times the forecast pre-tax profits and also because the net asset value, about £0·12 per share, was tiny. The reason for the high asking price being obtained lay in the growth prospects of the company, and the public evidently had confidence that the prospects of growth were good.

MANAGEMENT POLICIES

The fostering of a strong team spirit and sense of loyalty to the company among all employees is something to which the company gives a good deal of attention. When the company moved from Cheshunt to Hethel all employees were

Table 8.1 Growth of Lotus cars, 1964–70

	1964	1965	1966	1967	1968	1969	1970
Production:							
Lotus cars produced	1,195	1,234	1,519	1,985	3,048	4,506	3,373
Ford Lotus Cortina	567	1,118	986	—	—	—	—
	1,762	2,352	2,505	1,985	3,048	4,506	3,373
Group turnover £	1,573,000	2,030,000	2,156,000	2,803,000	4,443,000	5,285,000	4,932,000
Group pre-tax profit £	113,000	154,000	251,000	324,000	731,000	606,000	322,000
Net worth £	50,000	123,000	255,000	410,000	700,000	772,000	870,000
Total employees:							
average for year	396	426	465	521	618	865	684
Profit on net worth	226%	125%	98%	79%	104%	79%	37%
Profit on turnover	7·2%	7·6%	11·6%	11·5%	16·5%	11·5%	6·5%

asked whether they wanted to come. Ninety-five per cent of the management staff opted to move, and so also did over 50 per cent of the workforce as a whole. This indicates the strong sense of loyalty that has been developed in the company.

It is company policy to endeavour to maintain a high level of pride in standards of workmanship and the quality of the cars. The factory and offices display notices with slogans like 'Lotus Quality is your job' and 'Lotus Quality is the Best Salesman'; these are hung around the factory as reminders of the importance of the quality of the company's cars.

In 1970 a further important step was taken in the company's management policies. This was the introduction of a staff charter. The charter explicitly recognised that a business must provide a vocation and prosperity for its work people, together with a maximum return for its shareholders. Under the terms of the charter, all hourly paid employees were transferred to weekly staff status with improved rates of salary, staff benefits and participation in a quality bonus which further improved actual earnings. The company was able to provide these additional employees benefits through the improvements in productivity and quality which they effected.

CONCLUSION

It is sometimes said that the days are gone when an entrepreneur could start a business in a backyard with only a few pounds and build up a large enterprise. The success of Lotus cars shows that this is untrue, even in an industry apparently dominated by giant companies. There are always gaps in the market which it is possible for a small man to fill and Colin Chapman found one of them.

Of the various qualities that are needed by the entrepreneur, one of the most important is determination. Inevitably there are failures as well as successes, and the entrepreneur, like everyone else has to overcome the discouragements that inevitably follow from setbacks. As a motoring man, when things go badly Collin Chapman finds solace in a verse by the poet of the car world, Henry Austin:

> 'Then take this honey for the bitterest cup,
> There is no failure save in giving up,
> No real fall so long as one still tries,
> For seeming setbacks make the strong man wise,
> There's no defeat in truth save from within,
> Unless you're beaten there you're bound to win.'

9 Plastic Coatings

Plastic Coatings is a science-based company and was formed by Nigel Vinson in 1952. Nigel Vinson first became interested in the possibilities of plastics as a schoolboy. The school used to organise outings to go and see local factories, and on one occasion the boys went to see a local plastics factory. At this time plastic was a new product and Nigel Vinson was impressed by what he saw. He was already considering a career as an entrepreneur and this was when he first thought that if he went into business he might choose plastics.

After leaving school and completing military service Nigel Vinson decided firmly that he would make a career in business. His aim was to set up a business of his own and his chief motivation was the wish to be his own boss.

When he began to think about what kind of business to go into, he thought again of plastics. It seemed obvious that whatever branch of business you choose to try to make your fortune in, it is best to choose a growth one. There must be a better chance in a growth business, and plastics seemed to be an obvious growth industry. Having decided on the plastics industry, Nigel Vinson considered that it would first be best to get some experience by working as an employee in the business. First he tried to get into ICI and then into Bakelite (as it was called at that time); but both these companies turned him down. Then he went to what was then the British Industries Fair. There were a number of firms exhibiting, one of which was a plastics company. He walked on to the stand and said to the manager 'I'd like to join you', and the manager said 'All right, come and join us'. It was a small business and he started with him the following week.

Nigel Vinson worked for this firm a year, and while he was there he saw that there were constant enquiries for protecting metal. The firm could have done the jobs but they had so many other things to do that they never accepted them. Eventually, Vinson suggested to his boss that they might set up a fifty-fifty company to exploit these opportunities. The boss turned this suggestion down and so Vinson left to set up his own company. He had spotted a neglected corner of the market, one of the commonest roads to success in establishing a successful business.

FORMING THE COMPANY

One of the first things that has to be done in setting up a company is to decide what to call it. Having the right name can be quite important and it is useful to have a name that is simple and self-explanatory, so that everyone knows immediately what the company does. Plastic Coatings is an excellent name, since it tells people precisely and simply what the company does—it puts on plastic coatings.

Another important initial problem is premises. After a three months' search, Nigel Vinson found a Nissen hut in Guildford at £7 10s a week rent.

THE PRODUCT

The company's product was putting plastic on to metals. The advantages of plastic-coated metals are of course that in many cases a plastic coating is the cheapest way of preventing rust. The company's first product was the dish drainers that go on the draining boards of sink units. The company bought them in metal, dipped them in plastic to give them a plastic coating, and sold them. At that time plastic-coated dish drainers were being imported from the United States and Sweden. No one was making them in England, and there were a number of wirework manufacturers looking around for someone who would coat their wirework for them.

Nigel Vinson built the first piece of plant himself, with the aid of one man. During his year as an employee he had learned that it is often possible to build equipment cheaply.

L

He mixed $2\frac{1}{2}$ tons of concrete by hand for the foundation, and then built a machine, largely out of ex-war aircraft bits and pieces, to do the plastic dipping process. His former boss had a similar machine, but Vinson designed a more sophisticated and efficient machine for the job.

After the dish drainers had become established as a line, the new company moved into other things like bath racks, clothes airers and clothes horses. For all of these there is a very big market today. Twenty years later the company was still coating all of these and also supplying the raw material for them and plant for coating them.

None of Plastic Coatings' products have been novel. They had all been made previously of some more expensive material. Dish drainers and clothes horses had been made of wood and bath racks used to be chromium plated. The company's advantage was being able to produce these products more cheaply. There was a big opportunity with the growing market for dish-washing machines. Here the only wire that will stand up to detergents is stainless steel, and all the framework to hold the dishes in these dish-washers used to be made of plain stainless steel wire. Stainless steel is very difficult to weld easily, it is rough and scratches glasses, and it corrodes under detergents. Nigel Vinson went to a manufacturer, Parnell Yate, and said: 'You're now making your baskets from stainless steel, if you make them of mild steel, not only will the welds be much stronger, so you won't have the number of breakages on the welds which you are getting now, but you could make them for about a third of the price, because your raw material cost would be so much less; and we are now in a position to coat these baskets for you.' They accepted his offer and as a result they finished up with a product that was 25 per cent cheaper and considerably better.

As soon as an entrepreneur develops a new product, he is fairly quickly faced with competition. Plastic Coatings has a great deal of competition, but they were first in and have succeeded in keeping ahead of the competitors. Vinson has never found patents any use as a protection from competition. He has taken them out in two instances, and they've been a waste of time. The company's hold on the market depends entirely on being ahead of everybody else generally, and that means only three or four years ahead.

GROWTH OF THE COMPANY

When the company was started in 1952 it consisted of Nigel Vinson and a secretary. Vinson did the dipping himself. He took on assistance only when the order level justified it. This was at the point when there was work running at about £100 a week. The first jobs were to build the machine and try to get the orders.

After about three months the company had sufficient orders to justify taking on an assistant. Vinson took on a garage mechanic, which was useful because he was handy at repairing the machinery. This was what was needed, because if you have to send out for experts to come and repair equipment, then you will soon lose money.

After four years of existence, by 1956, Plastic Coatings had a staff of thirty and an annual turnover of £50,000. The company has grown steadily at around 17 to 20 per cent a year. It went public in 1969. By 1970 it had eight factories, a staff of 850 and an annual turnover of around £3 million.

FINANCE

It is generally necessary to have some capital for starting a business. In this respect Nigel Vinson was quite fortunate because he had come into £4,000 and he was able to put this sum into the company. But it was not strictly necessary for him to have this amount. He could have begun with about £1,000; it would have taken a bit longer to build the business up, but it would not have been a serious handicap.

The plastic coating business is a good one in that the work passes through the factory in a matter of hours, rather than months, so that the amount of money tied up in work in progress and stocks is absolutely minimal. When the company has obtained six weeks' credit from its suppliers, which could be obtained without any trouble once it had started to pay its bills, the whole thing became virtually self-financing by the suppliers giving more and more credit.

In addition, the company obtained overdraft facilities from one of the local banks. Plastic Coatings has never had any difficulty in getting a bank loan. It has found that provided the company is making profits and that the overdraft is turning over, or in other words the cash flow is effectively paying off the overdraft, the banks do not mind if the company continues in overdraft. They take the view that each year you're ploughing back something that notionally pays the overdraft off. In effect the business is getting bigger and Plastic Coatings' overdraft went up and up every year. But its overdraft has been roughly proportional to the turnover, so that the banks have only ever really loaned the company one year's money.

For its first six years Plastic Coatings relied entirely on internal financing from suppliers' credit, retained profits and bank overdraft. After six years Nigel Vinson wanted to expand the company further and needed some long-term money. He obtained this from the Industrial and Commercial Finance Corporation and in return he sold them 10 per cent of the shares. In 1969 Plastic Coatings was floated as a public company and 30 per cent of the shares were sold to the public. In 1971 Nigel Vinson sold his remaining shareholding to Imperial Tobacco for £4 million.

DIVERSIFICATION AND GROWTH

During the course of its development the company has developed a number of different sides of the plastic coatings business. The coating business uses essentially the same principle as the toffee-apple. You can do two things. Either you leave the coating on and protect the apple, or you can strip the toffee off and you've then got a moulding. Thus there are two sides to the business: the basic plastic coating side and the ancillary moulding, where instead of making a coating bond, the coating is deliberately released leaving a shape which follows the contour of the original article. The company is in the jobbing business and in this it quite often happens that it is doing so much work for a customer that he decides he wants to do it himself, because for practical purposes it eliminates transport and is more convenient. Plastic Coatings accepts that this is likely to happen and has always told its customers that should they want to do their own work, then the company will supply them with plant and would hope to supply them with raw material. In this way the company generally obtains a continuity of business, and although it does not make anywhere near as much in turnover terms when it sells raw material as when it actually does the work, at least it makes something out of it.

One of Plastic Coatings' new products is the all-plastic Wellington boot. It is a completely new technology and it makes a very attractive Wellington. The company employs its maintenance engineers building capital equipment. It finds that they enjoy the work. It is fulfilling for them to design and build new machinery. Nigel Vinson has personally taken a good deal of interest in the technological side of the business.

The company's major business in the early 1970s is the coating of street lampposts for the prevention of rust. Street lampposts used to be painted, but the cost of repainting is very high, involving both scaffolding and labour. Plastic Coatings coats them before they are erected. The concrete ones cannot be made tall enough, so there has been a big swing back to steel. There is a very big market there and at the company's Cheshire factory it coats poles up to 40 feet long. There is an international demand for this and the company has had both Japanese and Americans coming in to see the plant with a view to buying either the drawings or to letting Plastic Coatings build the plant for them.

DELEGATION OF RESPONSIBILITY TO MANAGERS AND FOREMEN

One of the things that Nigel Vinson has practised is the maximum delegation of responsibility to managers and foremen. In the company everything possible is done to encourage status—to make the foremen feel important, to make the junior manager know that his decisions matter, to make the letter-writer responsible for his letter. But while the company encourages the responsibility of the individual, it strictly discourages the creation of phoney barriers of class, such as signs saying 'No Workers Beyond this Point'.

It is still common in industry today to give office workers 'staff' status and to regard them as superior beings from a social and capability point of view. Vinson takes the view that this creates artificial social barriers which encourage an attitude of 'we' and 'they' and is fundamentally bad for the morale of a company.

But Vinson believes strongly in the importance of status. He tries to give all the junior managers and foremen the maximum amount of responsibility and privileges. He encourages them to take decisions and makes certain that all plans are communicated from the top downwards and not from the bottom upwards. They must know first what is happening. They have the right to hire and fire. But if a foreman makes a mistake Vinson deliberately does not support him through thick and thin. He is quite prepared to reverse the decision. He takes the view that although this may for a moment undermine that particular foreman's authority, it fosters the feeling that the company is fair. Where decisions that have been made wrongly have been reversed, it has generally been found that the foreman has learned and benefited from the experience.

It is company policy to ensure that its foreman and junior managers are paid more than those who work under them. They also get more in privileges, extra holidays, free use of telephones and so forth. All foremen and junior managers have keys to the factories in which they work to show that the company has trust in them.

All of them too are given the profit and loss figures of their particular department and this has proved of inestimable value. Vinson was somewhat hesitant when he first introduced it, as he felt it would develop a feeling of 'Look what the department has made today, hundreds of pounds, and I've only been paid a fiver'. The result has been quite the reverse. It is extraordinary what enthusiasm it has generated to beat the target figure, and how quickly a wrongly costed job is brought to the attention of the sales department. It has made people feel that they are really involved in the business of making the firm pay. They know their decisions count.

The company has encouraged its foremen and junior managers to take the maximum personal interest in their staff and not leave it all to the personnel officer. For whilst there are many problems of a legal and family nature that somebody fully experienced can best deal with, there are many little personal matters that require immediate attention. For instance, foremen have full authority to give people the day off at half pay if they consider that there is an overriding personal necessity to do so.

It may be felt that foremen may abuse this discretion. It has been found that occasionally they do but it is felt to be worth it because it brings into the works the human touch. Another way of humanising the business is that all heads of departments are circulated daily with the names of those in their department who have a birthday or whose anniversary it is of joining the firm—the first, second, tenth etc. year they have worked. Then when the departmental head goes around he can say 'Good morning Fred, happy birthday', or 'Good morning George, I can't see how you have stuck working in this firm for ten years, you must be crazy'. All this is done in an effort to personalise relations and to make people feel they matter. Vinson regards these small human touches as important and recalls an Americanism which says 'A smile is a curve which helps straighten out a lot of things'.

It may be thought that discipline breaks down under a system like this. The experience of Plastic Coatings has been that fair dealing does not lead to loose discipline; indeed, rather the reverse, relations are strengthened. A sloppily run firm is neither a happy firm nor an efficient one. Discipline is important, and by and large people like to work in an organisation where the discipline is fair but firm. A polite but firm 'will you?' carries far greater persuasion than 'you will'.

As part of the company's policy of encouraging responsibility, all letters leaving the firm are signed by name. Many firms still have in small print at the bottom of letters: 'All correspondence should be addressed to the firm and not to individuals'. What happens in fact when you phone that firm is that you study the typist's reference at the top ('DVS'), then you get on the phone to the telephonist and say 'Will you please put me through to your reference DVS', and eventually you get through to Mr David Smith. To hide behind anonymity does not encourage responsibility, rather the reverse. Somewhere along the line individuals have got to deal with problems, so it seems best to make that individual's responsibility clear from the very beginning. The company employs a number of other small techniques for increasing the personal responsibility of its staff. For example, if Mr Smith is wanted on the phone, instead of broadcasting 'Mr Smith is wanted on the phone please', make it certain that its telephonists broadcast 'Mr Smith to the nearest phone please, Mr Jones of the Ford Motor Company for you'. This does two things. First it gives Mr Smith a chance to think what it is that Mr Jones is probably calling him about, and secondly, it broadcasts through the entire works that the Ford Motor Company is calling for Mr Smith and subconsciously reminds everyone that it is the Ford Company that has placed one of the orders on which they are working. Vinson believes it is very important that people should constantly be reminded that their employer is not strictly the firm they are working for, but the firm for whom they are producing goods. He is the customer on whom their livelihood ultimately depends.

Another thing Plastic Coatings does is to make certain that its production planners, instead of being in a separate planning office from which they have to communicate to the manufacturing department concerned, have an office actually in the department for which they are responsible. They sit in the same office as the foreman in an air-conditioned and sound-proofed glass section. This has three very beneficial effects: they double up for the foreman when he is out, there is the minimum of delay in getting an answer to the customer, and last but not least, it brings the office directly onto the factory floor. The fall-out of information disseminates throughout the department and makes people conscious of what they are producing and for whom they are producing it.

Here again, the company's job cards are not just numbered but also named with the name of the customer. Also if a progress chaser or foreman makes a promise of delivery to the customer, he fills out a promise card which he signs. This commits him personally as the promiser, and gives a feeling of obligation in seeing that this promise is met. Copies of this card go to the section directly responsible for getting the work out, the inspection, despatch and other departments concerned. This personal involvement really seems to work, and the company generally finds that its promises are kept.

COMPANY MORALE

Nigel Vinson believes that one of the most important things in a company is to achieve a high level of morale among the workforce. Morale is the feeling that the company is a good one, that it works as a team in which all have an important part to play, that the management cares about the workers and that the workers care about the good of the firm.

There are various ways in which good morale can be achieved. In Plastic Coatings three have been found especially useful, and these are first a human relations policy, secondly financial incentives for productivity, and thirdly the provision of good promotion prospects for all workers.

HUMAN RELATIONS—INVOLVEMENT

Vinson recalls that in his first job he went into one factory, and as he walked along the corridor saw a notice 'No Workers Beyond this Point'. He felt his hackles rise in sheer repugnance against such a statement, and it was from this point that he became particularly conscious of so many of the self-inflicted and unnecessary social barriers that industry erects round itself.

The important thing is to build up feelings of involvement

and participation among the workers. It is essential to avoid any division into 'we' and 'they'. The problem of developing participation is to encourage people to think not of 'we' and 'they' but of 'our'.

Now if people are to feel they are genuinely participating, they must feel within themselves that their contributions count. One of management's most important jobs is to remember that people need to be recognised and to feel responsible, and that these needs must be satisfied by the maximum involvement.

To develop a feeling of involvement it is necessary to trust people. In Plastic Coatings a considerable effort is made to put information over. Nigel Vinson believes that the 'My door is always open, you can always come and chat' philosophy, while right in principle, often does not work well in practice. If you are going to make the effort to keep people informed, you have to make an active effort to disseminate information.

The company holds regular section meetings in the firm's time, where the entire section is addressed by the departmental manager who is their immediate boss. His position and photograph are clearly shown on the Organisation Tree, which is on the notice board. Where possible, and certainly no less than four times a year, he has with him one of the executive directors of the company. At these meetings the managers explain where the company is going, what expansion is planned next, and generally welcome the broadest discussion on day-to-day conditions, annual holidays, fringe benefits and all the myriad of problems on people's minds. The purpose of this is to ensure that none of the employees feel remote and out of touch with the managers who are taking the decisions that are affecting their lives.

At these meetings a real effort is made to make people profit-conscious. The managers explain that the only alternative to making a profit is making a loss and there is no happy state in between. It is further emphasised that profit is the only yardstick by which the viability of a concern can be judged.

Another of the company's methods of fostering good

human relations is by organising an annual 'Mums and Dads Night'. This is an open evening or afternoon, where anybody who works in the company can invite their relatives—boys and girls their parents, husbands their wives, etc. A general tour by the work people is felt to be beneficial in human terms, in relating the employees' work to his home life and friends, and equally important in informing everybody who works in the company exactly what the company does. This occasion includes films of the company's activities and a talk where the foreman of the department, or the manager, can tell the parent exactly what he thinks of his offspring and how he is doing. About 70 per cent of the staff come to these events and appear to enjoy them.

As part of the company's general policy of encouraging personal responsibility, an attempt is being made to move towards the concept of staff status for everybody. Nigel Vinson believes that the word 'staff' has come to lose its meaning in industrial terms, and now rather than describing everybody who works for an organisation it is associated with 'they'. It is part of the 'management and workers' philosophy which it is not desirable to perpetuate. Accordingly, Plastic Coatings has dropped the use of the term 'staff' and prefers, when talking about different categories of employees, to use the word 'grades'. This is essentially an attempt to eliminate the exclusiveness of the staff grade and to close the gap between 'them' and the factory workers.

Up-to-date attempts to take everybody off the clock below chargehand level and to abolish time-keeping have been disappointing. However, the company has abolished clocking-out and found that this has had a beneficial effect. Instead of people edging towards the clock and beginning to queue at one minute to five, they stay at their sections and in fact less time is lost than would be otherwise and a sense of obligation is growing. Another thing the company does is to try to make certain that small repair jobs and improvements are done quickly. Small breakdowns like a bolt missing off a machine or a key missing on a typewriter can cause aggravations out of all proportion to their size. It is company policy to encourage employees to point out these little maintenance problems and make certain that they are dealt with quickly. It is felt that it lowers the employee's morale to have to ask constantly for something to be put right, and for nothing to be done about it.

One of the most important aspects of work to an employee is his security. Employees are naturally concerned about this, and to achieve it in Plastic Coatings all employees who have worked in the company for more than a year are given a certificate of security of employment. It is a deliberately quite grand looking document which is issued formally by the company secretary. This lays out clearly the employee's rights under the Redundancy Act and clearly commits the company to further payments in the event of redundancy occurring through no fault of his own. It is felt that it is right to make this commitment as formal as possible, so that the employee knows that the matter has been most carefully considered.

A similar problem occurs with sickness. Plastic Coatings runs a sickness scheme which makes up an employee's pay to at least two-thirds of his basic wage. In addition to the sick scheme, there is a 'hard luck scheme', where if an employee has to take time off through no fault of his own, such as sickness of wife or child etc., the firm will help make up his pay to two-thirds, in exactly the same way as if he has been ill.

The company also operates a pensions scheme. In cases where the company can do substantially better than the state scheme, employees are contracted out. It is a contributory scheme with the employee and the company each paying 50 per cent of the contributions.

FINANCIAL INCENTIVES

Wage rates are fixed by a system of merit ratings. Some consideration has been given to piecework but the company has come down against it. Piecework gives rise to a number of problems, such as the reduction in labour mobility, the increase in scrap and the necessity of supervision, which often more than offset its apparent advantages.

Under the company's 'merit rating' system the head of a department can award increments of merit bonus to people who do exceptionally good work. The experience of the company has been that this does not lead to an attitude of mind of 'Why should he get more than I do?'. On the contrary, it makes the best men satisfied in knowing that they get more than the people who are not as good as they are.

Plastic Coatings also pays additional increments for length of service. The object of this policy is to reward loyalty to the company and to give the employees something to look forward to. Under the system an employee gets an increase in pay for every year he has worked in the company, up to a maximum of six years. This is paid in addition to the 'merit rating'. With increments for long service and merit an employee can be earning at least 30 per cent more for doing a particular job than somebody who has just walked in the door the day before.

In addition to this, the company also runs a monthly output profit-sharing bonus scheme. The problem with bonus schemes is that it is generally impossible to pay out a large additional slice of money, for the simple reason that there just is not enough profit made to enable the company to do so. Thus many bonus schemes yield the odd one or two pounds at the end of a month, which may have some beneficial effect but is not particularly impressive.

In Plastic Coatings the bonus scheme is payable as a percentage of salary, uniformly throughout the company, from teaboys in the office, to floor sweepers in the works, to general managers. It is an average bonus scheme, and no matter where the profit is made throughout the company, and from whichever division it comes, it is spread uniformly. This is done to prevent unnecessary rivalry or hogging of work between the factories.

The bonus is based on productivity. At the end of each year the company calculates the total wages paid as a percentage of total sales. For example, this could come to 30 per cent and this is used as a base figure for the following year. Where in any month the total wages to sales are say 27 per cent, an improvement in terms of productivity, the factor of 3 is multiplied by a constant to give a proportional increase in people's monthly pay. The aim is that at the end of a successful and profitable year some three weeks' extra pay is distributed overall. If in the next month the wages to sales figure rose to say 33 per cent, a sign of falling productivity, a negative bonus would be declared which would be deducted. Thus, if the sales department negotiate a good price the bonus goes up, if the sales department negotiate a bad price and the margin is very thin the bonus goes down. Equally, if the works produce the goods faster than anticipated the bonus goes up but alternatively if there is a high reject factor and extra work involved, the bonus goes down. In most schemes there is no fund from which to make deductions in the event of a loss being made. Plastic Coatings gets over this problem by crediting the bonus amount monthly to people's 'bonus account'. Thus on the first payday of each month every employee receives a chit which reads, say, as follows:

> Your bonus for last month was   £ 6·71
> Your bonus account now stands at   £28·18

This makes the carrot quickly follow the month of effort and apparently makes an impact of real significance.

Thus, in non-profit-making months, such as those in which most of the annual holidays fall, or in slack trading over Christmas, the individual's bonus is reduced. It is felt that this is salutary. If the bonus was always plus and never minus, it would be taken for granted. In a genuine profit-sharing scheme, people should share in the losses as well as the profits. Of course there are moans in the months when there are deductions but this is probably a healthy sign: it shows that people are really aware of what is going on. The bonus is paid out twice annually. One-third is paid just before the annual holidays in the summer, so that a small bonus is carried forward afterwards from which deductions can be made if necessary, and the remaining two-thirds a fortnight before Christmas. If any member of the company hands in his notice, or has to be dismissed for misbehaviour at any time throughout the year, he forfeits his bonus. This is not penalisation but to compensate for the loss of profit caused by the disrupture of his departure. This is quite clearly known by everybody. It helps to reinforce the company's philosophy that the bonus should not be expected as a right but is the result of a genuine participation in the success of the firm.

If at any time throughout the year a man is given a rise, either as a merit award or through promotion, this is not done casually on the floor of the factory, but a real feature is made of it in the manager's office. The object here is to impress on the employee that his services to the company are valued.

PROMOTION FROM INSIDE THE COMPANY

On the question of promotion it is company policy to promote from inside the company wherever possible. In order to give people a broad training the company operates a policy of posting many of its employees between factories, not only permanently but for the occasional week and even the occasional day. It is felt that where possible people need to be taken off routine jobs and given variety in their lives. This policy has been received with remarkable enthusiasm. Of course it is not always possible to find the man that is needed from within the organisation, but when advertising is necessary it is company policy to make certain that before an advertisement appears in the local press, it goes up on the notice board for all to see at least the day before. The object of this is to ensure that the employees are kept informed about the company from the inside and not from the outside.

In this account a good deal of space has been devoted to the question of the human relations policies pursued in Plastic Coatings. The reason for this is that Nigel Vinson has taken considerable trouble over his company's relations and this has undoubtedly been an important element in the growth of this exceptionally successful company.